Victor M. Rose

**Ross' Texas Brigade**

Victor M. Rose

**Ross' Texas Brigade**

ISBN/EAN: 9783744685948

Printed in Europe, USA, Canada, Australia, Japan

Cover: Foto ©ninafisch / pixelio.de

More available books at **www.hansebooks.com**

# ROSS'
# TEXAS BRIGADE.

BEING A

NARRATIVE OF EVENTS CONNECTED WITH ITS SERVICE IN THE LATE WAR BETWEEN THE STATES.

---

BY VICTOR M. ROSE.

*"CONCLAMATUM EST."*

---

LOUISVILLE, KY.
PRINTED AT THE COURIER-JOURNAL BOOK AND JOB ROOMS.
1881.

TO THE

HERO PATRIOT

**GENERAL L. S. ROSS,**

THE CHEVALIER BAYARD OF THE WESTERN ARMIES

OF THE CONFEDERATE STATES OF AMERICA, UNDER WHOSE

ABLE LEADERSHIP THE TEXAS BRIGADE WON

ITS JUSTLY MERITED RENOWN,

THESE PAGES ARE GRATE-

FULLY INSCRIBED BY HIS

FRIEND AND COMRADE

THE AUTHOR.

Entered according to Act of Congress, in the year 1881, by
THE COURIER-JOURNAL COMPANY,
in the Office of the Librarian of Congress, at Washington, D. C

# CONTENTS.

Salutatory . . . . . . . . . . . . . . . . . . . . . . . . . . . . . . . . 5
Chapter I.—Organization of the Third Regiment Texas Cavalry—March to Missouri—Battle of Oak Hills—Incidents, etc. . . . . . . . . . 13
Chapter II.—Arrival of the Sixth Texas Cavalry—Incidents of the Campaign—Mabry and Johnson's Gallant Fight—Biographical Sketch of Colonel Greer . . . . . . . . . . . . . . . . . . . . . . . . . . . 34
Chapter III.—Death of Captain Harris—Battle of Chustenahlah—Winterquarters—Kindness of Mrs. Greer, etc. . . . . . . . . . . . . . . . 42
Chapter IV.—Van Dorn Arrives and Assumes Command—Elk Horn—Death of McCulloch and McIntosh—Incidents, etc. . . . . . . . 53
Chapter V.—Retreat from Elk Horn—Rescue of Artillery—Embarkation at Duvall's Bluff—Memphis—Corinth—Etc., etc. . . . . . . . . 63
Chapter VI.—Battle of Iuka . . . . . . . . . . . . . . . . . . . . . . . 69
Chapter VII.—Battle at Oakland—Capture of Holly Springs . . . . . . 78
Chapter VIII.—The Campaign in Tennessee—Death of General Van Dorn—Campaign in Mississippi, etc. . . . . . . . . . . . . . . . . . . 98
Chapter IX.—The Beginning of the End . . . . . . . . . . . . . . . . . 114
Biographical Sketch of General John S. Griffith . . . . . . . . . . . . 123
Biographical Sketch of Hon. O. N. Hollingsworth . . . . . . . . . . . 138
Biographical Sketch of Colonel Elkanah Greer . . . . . . . . . . . . . 140
Biographical Sketch of Colonel H. P. Mabry . . . . . . . . . . . . . . 142
Biographical Sketch of General J. W. Whitfield . . . . . . . . . . . . 147
Biographical Sketch of Colonel D. W. Jones . . . . . . . . . . . . . . 149
Biographical Sketch of Colonel Jack Wharton . . . . . . . . . . . . . 151
Biographical Sketch of Colonel John H. Broocks . . . . . . . . . . . . 153
Biographical Sketch of General Laurence Sullivan Ross . . . . . . . . 157
Battle of the Wichita—The Rescue of Lizzie Ross from Captivity . . . 175
Reminiscences of Camp Chase . . . . . . . . . . . . . . . . . . . . . . 179
The South . . . . . . . . . . . . . . . . . . . . . . . . . . . . . . . . 185

# SALUTATORY.

Victor Hugo says: "Destiny entertains a purpose. It watches mysteriously over the future historian. It allows him to mingle with exterminations and carnages, but it does not allow him to die, because it wishes him to relate them." Be this as it may, certainly an actor in the scenes he describes should be allowed to possess advantages in the narration of the incidents not possessed by one not so connected.

The author was an actor in most of the events portrayed, and, in addition thereto, he has had the fraternal co-operation of his old comrades—from the commanders down—in the prosecution of this "labor of love."

During the year 1863, Captain Rufus F. Dunn, Company F, Third Regiment Texas Cavalry, was, on account of his feeble health, detailed from operations in the field to write a history of the operations of Ross' Texas Brigade; which design, as the following extract from a letter of General Ross shows, was immediately defeated by the death of Captain Dunn, and permanently impaired by the loss of documentary data, trophies, etc., mentioned. The extract in question reads: "Captain Dunn, whose health had failed, was detailed to write a full and accurate history of the brigade, and I furnished him with all necessary data, orders, papers, etc., to render his duty of easy compliance; but, unfortunately, he died in Alabama, and I received this information simultaneously with the intelligence that my trunk and private papers entrusted to his care had fallen into the hands of the enemy. In my trunk was found twenty stands of colors, and other trophies that we had captured from the Federals."

After many efforts to ascertain the whereabouts of Mrs. Dunn, success was attained in 1878. This estimable lady, Mrs. Parmelia A. Dunn, of Providence, Pickens county, Ala., had, through all these weary years of war and licentious misrule, guarded with fidelity the trust imposed upon her by her dying husband's injunction, and preserved, unscathed, through pillage and sack, the precious manuscript upon which his last care had been expended. To this Cornelia of the South, the surviving comrades of her lamented husband tender their heartfelt thanks.

It is regretted that the orders and other papers alluded to in General Ross' letter were not recovered. Hence, much of the material used has been drawn from other sources; generally, from the memories of surviving members of the command, a necessity that caused delay, and exacted much patience on the part of the author in arranging the many conflicting statements that had grown with time. But it is safe to assert that nothing but absolute truth has been entered on these pages; not the whole truth, for that, alas! may never now be told.

The treatment of a subject should always reflect the object sought to be attained without necessitating any special revelation in regard thereto. In this narrative, called for by the dictates of simple justice to the living and dead, a vindication of their motives is essayed by a brief recapitulation of their services in camp and field. Their courage and chivalry, their heroic fortitude, and manly fidelity to a hopeless cause need no vindication. And, if any were needed, we would turn to the childhood home of the English tongue—the cradle of the Anglo-Norman race—and find such vindications as the eloquent extract which is here reproduced from the columns of the London *Standard*, in the year 1878, when the South was stricken by that pestilential scourge of the tropics—yellow fever: "The younger among us can not, perhaps, remember the keen, warm sympathy with which the English of 1861–5 witnessed the heroic struggle maintained by their Southern kinsmen against six-fold odds of numbers, and odds of position, resources, vantage ground, simply incalculable. Even those who, from sympathy with the Northern States were unfavorable to the cause of a great nation revolting against a real tyranny, could not but feel proud of our near kinship with that incomparable soldiery—so designated by their enemies—which, on fifty battle-fields, maintained such a contest as no other race has ever, in modern times, maintained; and, at last, when all hope was gone, held for six months, with 45,000 against 150,000, a slender line of earth-works thirty miles in length; who marched out 28,000 strong, and after six days' retreat in front of a countless cavalry, and overwhelming artillery and infantry pressing them on all sides, surrendered, at last, but 8,000 bayonets and sabers. It is this people, the flower and pride of the great English race, upon whom a more terrible, a more merciless enemy has now fallen. There can be now no division of sympathy, as there is no passion to excite and keep up the courage needed for the occasion. Yet the men and women of the South are true to the old tradition. Her youth volunteer to serve and die in the streets of plague-stricken cities, as readily as they went forth, boys and grey-haired men, to meet the threatened surprise of Petersburg—as they volunteered to charge again and again the cannon-crowned heights of Gettysburg, and to enrich with their blood, and honor with the name of a new victory, every field around Richmond. Their sisters, wives, mothers, and daughters, are doing and suffering now as they suffered from famine, disease, incessant anxiety, and alarm, throughout the four years of the civil war. There may be among the various nations of the Aryan family one or two who would claim that they could have furnished troops like those which followed Lee and Johnston, Stuart and 'Stonewall' Jackson; but we doubt whether there be one race beside our own that could send forth its children by hundreds to face, in towns desolated by yellow fever, the horror of a nurse's life and the imminent terror of a martyr's death." And, finally, it is a solemn duty that the survivors owe to their fallen comrades to leave a truthful record of their deeds, upon which shall be predicated the judgment of posterity.

It is to such works as this that the future historian of the American sectional war must have recourse for facts; for the truth of history must rest upon the statements of those who were contemporaneous with the events they detail. Were this, then, the sole object, no further reason would be necessary for the appearance of the work. "Returning justice lifts aloft her scale," and the fame of the Confederate soldier has risen far above the aspersions and calumnies that were sought to be cast upon it; and the descendants of Ross' invincible rangers will piously treasure the record of their services as an invaluable souvenir, and transmit it as an heir-loom to their remotest posterity. And to that record the youth of the coming generation will point with pride, and say: "My grandsire fought with Ross at Elk Horn, Iuka, Corinth, Atlanta, and the hundred other fields upon which the 'Old Brigade' signalized itself!" They will rejoice over the recital of our victories, and shed tears over the story of our reverses; and, with the conclusion of the final chapter, over which the somber legend—"*Conclamatum est*"—hangs like a funeral pall, they will close the volume with Christian resignation, breathing in their hearts the silent prayer: "Thy will, O God, be done!"

Indeed, the fame of the Confederate soldier is secure wherever the sway of Southern woman's influence is felt; and if, in succeeding generations, this land gives birth to as noble women as those who sacrificed every thing for the cause of Dixie, the treasure of his reputation could be consigned to no safer guardianship. Though out of place, perhaps, we can not refrain from paying this merited tribute to the matchless women of the South. It was theirs to wish God-speed to father, husband, brother, son, departing for the conflict where the valley was red. And though the yearnings of nature filled their hearts to bursting, while dark forebodings as to the fate of the loved one setting out for the front rose like a nightmare on the mind, yet they *spoke* but words of encouragement and hope. Many a mother bid her only son adieu with the sentiment of the Spartan matron holding sway in her heart, though the loving lips refused to utter it: "Take this shield, my son, and bear it back to me thyself, or be borne upon it!" Who rejoiced like they at our ephemeral triumphs? Who shed as bitter tears over our losses and defeats? Their trust in the God of hosts was sublime, and when craven manhood forsook his colors in despair, at the surrender of Vicksburg, and the melting away of Lee's lines before Petersburg, the star of their faith shone still with a constancy akin to its celestial birth, and nothing but the irrefragible evidence itself of the utter subversion of the ill-fated Confederacy, and the surrender of its armies, served to relax their ardor and exertions for the doomed cause. And then, reading upon the lowering clouds of the future the death-knell of all their cherished hopes, they turned to the past, upon angelic missions, among the unlettered graves of their fallen countrymen, and the stranger reads, with a thrill of pleasure, of the ministrations of these angels on earth, as each returning May brings its tributes of flowers for "Decoration Day."

In this peerless sisterhood, our country recognizes its greatest worth; and happy our manhood, our chivalry, to ever kneel as votaries at that pure shrine. A cause that is upheld by such spotless advocates can not be a bad cause. The doctrines of hell are not propagated by evangels of mercy. But it was the inscrutable will of

Providence that their prayers should be of none avail, as this immutable administration had before decreed the elimination of empires from the map of the world.

The genius of Hannibal, the prowess of his legions, and the sacrifices of his devoted countrywomen in defense of right, could not avert the fate of Carthage. The sympathies of the world are now with dismantled Carthagena; and, compared with the dubious ray of starlight that illumines the name of Scipio, Hannibal's is a sunburst of refulgence. And now, when we remember the tragic fate that has overtaken many of those fanatics who preached the doctrine of hate against the South, we recall the story of the Roman victor skulking amid the ruins of his subjugated rival.

The fact is attested by the holy Scriptures that nations are but instrumentalities in the hands of God for the execution of His will upon earth. Thus, commencing with the Babylonian Empire, we descend, by links of nations, down the chain of time, according to interpretation of the writings of the Prophet Daniel, to the Roman and Ottoman Empires. The Chaldean, Assyrian, Medo-Persian, Macedonian, Roman, and Turkish, were each but an instrument in His hands—a medium through which to effect his designs in regard to the advancement of civilization, and the melioration of the condition of mankind. The Roman power was the great disseminator of the truths of Christianity. Being mistress of almost the whole of the known earth when Constantine embraced the true religion, it became but a question of mere time when the gospel should reach, through Roman intercourse, every province and region penetrated for commerce, curiosity, or conquest. It was for this that the palladins of Rome were allowed to subjugate a world. No earthly puissance could stay the onward tramp of the Roman legion in thus executing the will of Him on high. To this the Scipios and Cæsars involuntarily contributed until Titus was suffered to raze the walls of Jerusalem to the ground, and, in so doing, he only emphasized the period to the "Old Dispensation." The "New Covenant" was then being taught by the "fishers of Galilee." And so is the United States designed by Omnipotence to serve some great purpose in the administration of His will among the peoples of earth. Of course, all speculation as to that purpose is futile. But with the Government brought back to the pure principles of the Constitution, through that sentiment of the equality of man, under our free institutions, it is thought the zenith of social and political excellence can be attained. And, in the not very distant future, its effect will be remarked upon the monarchical governments of Europe. Indeed, its effect is felt there now, and has been since their desire to emulate us caused the French to behead their king. Thus, American influence, giving hope to the oppressed of Europe, will go forth as the great evangel of liberty, and subjugate more nations to truth and happiness than were conquered by all the legions of Rome. And, in the fulfillment of this high destiny, the sagacity of Lee and Johnston, Beauregard and Jackson, and the valor and endurance of their men, was futile. But as the last sigh of the Moor awakes sympathy throughout Christendom for the doomed race whose lofty deeds of daring could not retain for them the rich conquest of Grenada, so, in aftertimes, the "Lost Cause" will gather about its mystic legends a weird tissue of romance and poetry, which, toned and mellowed by age, will eventually develop itself into an epic like the "Cid" or "Henriade." But it is only for the atom of an abstract idea that this apotheosis is invoked by the future Homer. For, barring property, the South lost nothing by the war that is not being regained in the Senate. Her people have adapted themselves to the new order of things, and, hand in hand with the honest Democracy of the West and East, are determined to stand by the rock of the Constitution as vigilant sentinels on the bulwarks of liberty. Of course, in this estimation, our priceless dead are not included. Their loss was incalculable.

The thanks of the author are due, for prompt assistance, and gratefully tendered, to

Mrs. PARMELIA A. DUNN, Providence, Pickens county, Ala.; J. WYLIE MONTGOMERY, Sheriff Rains county, Texas; General L. S. ROSS, Waco, McLennan county, Texas; E. A. KELLOGG, Secretary Ross' Brigade Association, Sulphur Springs, Hopkins county, Texas; Lieutenant DAN. H. ALLEY, Jefferson, Marion county, Texas; Major J. W. DOWNS, of the Waco *Examiner and Patron;* Captain JOHN GERMANY, Lieutenant S. B. BARRON, L. FOWLER, Colonel W. B. SIMS, Captain SID. S. JOHNSTON, BEN. A. LONG, J. B. LONG, Captain T. J. TOWLS, Camden, Van Zandt county, Texas; T. J. GEE, Captain H. P. TEAGUE, I. E. KELLIE, SCOTT GOODSEL, and other friends, whose kindness is none the less appreciated because their names do not readily occur at this writing.

And now, but little more remains to be said, in this connection, ere the "narrative" is allowed to speak for itself; whether in a manner commendable to those whose approbation the author is desirous of gaining, or not, the result will demonstrate. He did not regard himself as at all *peculiarly* fitted for the task, and there are, doubtless, many others of his comrades who could have performed the work in a much more satisfactory manner. But one long decade had passed since the colors of the Brigade had been forever furled, and another well on its way, and no movement had been set on foot to rescue from oblivion the record of a command as rich in all the material treasured by valor, devotion, and chivalry, as ever graced the pages of history.

Twenty years ago, a friendless wanderer, of eighteen years of age, the writer cast his fortunes with them, and—call them rebels and traitors, revile the cause of the South as much as you will—he is prouder of his course, during those four years, than of any other period of his life. There be some who regard PRINCIPLE as of infinitely more value than the catch-words of expediency and policy. There be some who have not "bowed the pliant hinges of the knee that thrift might follow fawning," and to such proud spirits, "who would break, but never bend," the author tenders the result of his labors. V. M. R.

VICTORIA, TEXAS, OCTOBER, 1880.

# A NARRATIVE

OF THE

## SERVICES OF ROSS' TEXAS BRIGADE OF CAVALRY, IN THE LATE WAR BETWEEN THE STATES.

---

> "Rebellion! Foul, dishonoring word,
> Whose wrongful blight so oft' has stained
> The holiest cause that tongue or sword
> Of mortal ever lost or gained;
> How many a spirit born to bless
> Hath sunk beneath that withering name,
> Whom but a day's—an hour's—success
> Had wafted to eternal fame!"

"The noblest body of men that ever bared their breasts in defense of a loved land!"—*General L. S. Ross.*

"The flower and the pride of the Army of the West!"—*General Earl Van Dorn.*

---

## CHAPTER I.

ORGANIZATION OF THE THIRD REGIMENT TEXAS CAVALRY—MARCH TO MISSOURI—BATTLE OF OAK HILLS—INCIDENTS, ETC.

The year of grace one thousand eight hundred and sixty-one dawned amidst the most portentious clouds that had ever lowered above the political horizon of America since the stormy period in which the sovereignty of the STATES had their birth, nearly one hundred years before.

Abraham Lincoln had been elected President of the United States by the suffrages of a sectional party whose only vitality and power of cohesion consisted of antagonism against the South and her most cherished principles and institutions; and his induction into the high office was construed by the people of that devoted section as the beginning of the "irrepressible conflict," so long and so often elaborated by Mr. Seward, amid the approving cheers of delighted Northern audiences.

The declaration of Mr. Lincoln himself, that "this country could not remain half slave and half free," had always been regarded south of "Mason and Dixon's line" as a declaration of war; and, now that the aggressive and fanatical Northern Republicans had, by taking advantage of the suicidal folly of the Democratic party, placed themselves in a position to give weight to the declaration, the South recognized the only alternative but submission, left her, and reluctantly accepted the saucy gage of battle thrown, as a forced tender, by her fanatical foe, and proceeded to stake her all upon the brutal arbitrament of arms—a tribunal through whose precedents of unwritten law flow the turbid pollutions of Might and Butchery, and not the limpid stream of Right and Justice—relying, with sublime confidence, upon the justice of her cause and the valor of her sons.

But it is not our province, here, to recapitulate all those causes that precipitated the tempest of war upon our unhappy country. Suffice it to say, that the sectional administration at Washington gave the South no alternative. Mr. Lincoln and his advisers affected to regard secession, *per se*, as a declaration of war, and the Confederate Government only obeyed the dictates of prudence and reason in anticipating the storm by commencing a vigorous attack upon Fort Sumpter. The first gun on that occasion met an affirmative response from the hearts of nearly all the people of the South, as it also inflamed the rage of those at the North. All hopes of a compromise were now at an end; the line of demarcation was drawn; the work of pacific statesmen had ceased, that of the turbulent soldier was to begin; and, in the South, many original Unionists now accepted the situation of affairs, and cast their lots with their States and people.

It is supposed there are traitors and tories to every cause, and though that of "Dixie" was no exception to the general rule, in the Southern States, properly so styled, there were probably fewer of this nefarious class, *at the beginning*, than ever appeared in any revolution of like proportions and radical character. We say that this was so at the beginning. Degraded human nature never struggles to oppose the flood-tide that promises success. Even venal prosperity never lacks for servile minions to chant its pæans in tones of adulation. And many original secessionists underwent a moderation of their fire-eating proclivities with each Southern reverse, until, with that climax of catastrophes at Appomattox, they had completed the entire circle, and hailed the coming Yankees as original "Houston Union men." Inquisitive reader, don't ask to glance even at the roll of this Legion of Dishonor. Many now reside in palatial residences, and are families of *influence*—yet they made the poor, bleeding corse of the assassinated Confederacy, the stepping-stone to wealth, position, and power. The tocsin of war met a prompt, affirmative response, and every hamlet, village, and city was soon the scene of warlike preparation. The best elements of society were the first to volunteer. Youth, ever ardent, was conspicuous by its numbers; and schools and colleges dismissed their classes to swell the ranks of the embryo army. And right here, let the fact be recorded, that the best, the bravest, the hardiest, and less complaining soldiers were mere boys from sixteen to twenty years of age.

This period was pre-eminently *the* era of the parlor knight. West Pointers, who had never seen West Point, turned up whenever occasion required it. Scarred veterans from Nicaraugua sprung up as if by magic, and the author, alone, formed the personal acquaintance of at least twelve hundred survivors of the immortal six hundred who charged at Balaklava. Thus, every cross-roads store, where ardent spirits were kept, could boast its own live military man to perfect its "Beauregard Rifles," or "Jeff. Davis Grays," in the manual of arms and evolutions of the line. Whatever became of these "Major Savages," "Colonel Desperades," and "General Seviers"—pronounced "Severe"—is not positively known. It is thought their ardor moderated just before the time for marching, and that they subsequently formed a portion of that delectable fraction of our population who contributed so much to advance the cause through their arduous labors in smuggling cotton to the Yankees. Some ensconsed themselves in bomb-proofs about the Quartermaster and the Commissary Departments; while others developed alarming symptoms of disease that found, in the last shots fired, a speedy and radical cure.

At this time, too, the latent fact was revealed that many an old plodding citizen was a real military strategist. Such "natural-born generals" would gather an admiring crowd upon the street corners, and proceed to demonstrate with what ease Washington City could be captured. We never stopped short of the capital in those brave old days; and, perhaps, had the tide been taken just here at the flood, by a dashing leader, the capture of Washington could have been effected. Who knows? The author remembers ascending Red river in the month of May, 1861, fresh from his studies at Centenary College, and anxious to reach his native State and join a company before the war was over; for the eloquent "stump" statesmen did not hesitate to affirm that the end of thirty days would witness the close of the fifth act of the serio-comic drama. On board the same steamboat —the "Texas"—were Colonel Elkanah Greer and Captain Harris, both just from Montgomery, Alabama, the seat of the Provisional Government of the Confederate States, with their commissions.

Colonel Greer, immediately upon his arrival in Texas, issued a call for men, and designated Dallas as the point of rendezvous. The various companies soon arrived, and were mustered into the Confederate service for the period of "one year, unless sooner discharged;" so little did we comprehend the magnitude or duration of the struggle into which we were entering! Those words seemed a bitter sarcasm when twelve months afterward we were sworn in again, without invitation, "for three years, or the war."

The regiment was organized on the 13th of June, 1861, and as two other regiments had been raised in the State (for frontier protection), this was styled the Third Regiment of Texas Cavalry. Walter P. Lane, of Harrison county, was elected Lieutenant-Colonel, and G. W. Chilton, of Smith county, was elected Major.

The following companies composed the regiment:

Co. A, Harrison county, T. W. Winston, Captain.
Co. B, Rusk county, R. H. Cumby, Captain.
Co. C, Cherokee county, Frank Taylor, Captain.
Co. D, Hunt county, —— Hale, Captain.
Co. E, Shelby county, D. M. Short, Captain.
Co. F, Kaufman county, Isham Chisholm, Captain.
Co. G, Marion county, H. P. Mabry, Captain.
Co. H, Wood County, Johnson Russell, Captain.
Co. I, Cass county, William Bryan, Captain.
Co. K, Smith county, David Gaines, Captain.

Captain Harris had previously received his commission as Quartermaster; and Captain Armstrong, of Company B, was appointed Commissary of Subsistence. Lieutenant M. D. Ector received the appointment of Adjutant. Dr. Wallace McDougal, of Company C, was appointed Surgeon, and Dr. Daniel Shaw, of Company B, Assistant Surgeon. Abner Rogers, Company G, was named Sergeant-Major. The companies averaged something over one hundred men each, and the regiment thus organized was probably 1,200 strong.

The hospitality of the good citizens of Dallas must not be passed over in silence. Each citizen vied with his neighbor in the warmth of his reception of the various companies; and, finally, a mammoth collation was spread, consisting of all the delicacies of the season, by the patriotic and liberal people, around which the soldiers were formed in line and "invited" to charge. The Hon. R. B. Hubbard and Major G. W. Chilton improved this occasion of good cheer by the delivery of eloquent and patriotic speeches to the citizens and soldiers.

Our stay at Dallas was protracted by the non-arrival of the wagon-train, with arms, from San Antonio, until July 6th. Captain John J. Good had organized an artillery company at Dallas, which was attached to the regiment, and, with it, took up the line of march, on July 9, 1861, for the scene of operations in Missouri. In the MS. of my lamented predecessor in this work, I find that many of the ardent youth of the regiment had become smitten with the charms of the Dallas fair, and tore themselves away from the parting scene with reluctance, hugging the cheering hope of a sacred tryst when the cruel war was over. Alas! how many manly forms came not to the long looked-for re-union! Through tempest and storm, they were true to their troth; and go, maidens, who plighted your vows with the young heroes, to the lines of Corinth, Iuka, Oak Hills, Atlanta, Elk Horn, and where the forlorn hope led the hazardous escalade, you'll find them "sleeping the sleep that knows no waking" on "this side of the river." "No useless coffins enclose their breasts." No marble shafts point the pilgrim's steps to the hero-patriots' tombs. Their old, worn blankets were their only shroud; for the weary and struggling Confederacy, stabbed before and behind, was too poor to bury the patriot that she was unable to feed, and fell, herself, a murdered power, as much in the house of her *friends*, as by the hands of her enemies.

The arms received by the regiment were of a very inferior quality— old United States carbines, shot-guns, squirrel rifles, etc. Company A was partially armed with Colt's revolving rifles and six-shooters, while two companies received no arms until within the borders of

Arkansas. In arms and ammunition, we certainly were no match for the enemy, who had an abundance of weapons of the latest improvement. Our wagon-train consisted of United States wagons, captured at San Antonio, and the mules bore upon their flesh the plain imprint of Uncle Sam's brand. Even the Mexican teamsters simply continued the service in the Confederate army which they did not terminate in the United States army. An idea may be had of the kind of work the average Texas soldier imagined he would be called upon to perform in battle, by the huge knives carried by many. Some of these knives were three feet long, and heavy enough to cleave the skull of a mailed knight through helmet and all. I think they were never used in the butchery of the Yankees, and, ere the close of the first year's service, were discarded altogether. But great was the confidence of the Texas soldier in his own prowess. To whip the Yankees, five to one, was considered the minimum of good fighting, and they seldom encountered on the field a less superiority of numbers; and this was by no means the greatest advantage possessed by the Union forces over their adversaries. Yet the Southern Cross, time and again, led them to victory, which, alas, was never improved; and their deeds justify the assertion, that, with other counsels at the head of affairs, they would have proven victorious in the end. In fact, they were invincible against any power save that brutal grinding away by attrition, which the enemy was forced to adopt, and decline the combat on the open field, man to man.

Those were brave old days, we have said, and State Sovereignty cropped out on all occasions. To us, Texas was the "nation;" to her alone we owed allegiance. We were *allied* with the other Southern States, not indissolubly *joined*. Each company had a flag, and, in addition to its alphabetical designation, bore some other name suggested by the spirit of the times. Thus, Company A was the "Texas Hunters;" Company G, the "Dead-Shot Rangers," etc.

The regiment proceeded on its march, without incident, until the Red river was reached. We crossed at Colbert's Ferry into the Choctaw Nation, and encamped about a mile beyond. The river was quite low when the men and horses were ferried over. The wagon-train was leisurely crossing, the sky above was without the fleck of a cloud, when suddenly was heard the distant murmur of a coming rise; the murmur deepened into an ominous roar, as the angry waters were precipitated down the mountains, and the flood was upon us. In the brief period of thirty minutes, the swollen torrent reached from bank to bank, and it was with difficulty that the train was saved; indeed, Captain Dunn's MS. records the loss of one or two wagons.

We found our Choctaw allies abreast of the times, and earnestly preparing for war. This people were not behind their Texan compatriots in their hospitality to the men of the regiment, and numbers —men, women, and children—flocked to the camp to see the "warriors." And as the Choctaws were, so were the Creeks, Cherokees, and Chickasaws. Let the record here, once for all, suffice for each and every one of these noble tribes. We brought the conflict upon them, and involved them in the common ruin that overwhelmed us both; but as long as a tattered Confederate flag fluttered in the breeze, these "untutored children of the forest" rallied beneath its folds, with unabated fealty to the cause of the South. But if it be imagined that they are all literally untutored, the fact will not have been attained. To illustrate: One day, in the Cherokee Nation, a number of men dining at the residence of a prominent citizen, whose daughter, a young and beautiful girl, presided at the head of the table. A gallant young officer was profuse in his compliments to the pretty and intelligent girl. He finally declared that she bore a striking resemblance to the portraits of Anne of Austria, including, even, the world-renowned pouting lips, with their slight vermilion tinge. The young lady, not at all abashed by this comparison with the royal Anne, replied: "While I may not boast a regal, or even a patrician descent, I can claim that the blood of three of the most noble nations on earth courses through my veins—the Cherokee, the Creek, and the American." And this was delivered with a graceful toss of the head that would have done honor to fair Gabrielle d'Estrees, whose siren charms seduced France's greatest king from the path of honor, virtue, and duty.

*En route* for Fort Smith, Arkansas—the country was fertile, well watered and timbered. Near Big Blue, we passed through a beautiful little Cherokee village, amid the "vivas" of the men, and the smiles and waving of handkerchiefs by the ladies—the latter of whom presented the Colonel with a regimental flag. From the Big Blue to the Porto, a distance of ten miles, is a hilly, rocky, and broken country.

Here was encamped Colonel Cooper's Indian regiment, and we had the pleasure of witnessing a war-dance one evening. A tree, about six or ten inches in diameter, was denuded of its bark to a height of eight feet, and around this "war-pole" the warriors danced, chanting a deep, guttural, and monotonous drawl the while. The faces of the men were hideously painted, and they were arrayed in habiliments so fantastic that Harlequin himself would have been in the height of fashion. In the dubious moonlight, their weird figures seemed like some phantasm, while the cadence of the low and monotonous chant almost lulled the hearer into a lethargy. When the shrill war-whoop sounds from a single throat, echoed and re-echoed by the rocks and hills, startling the eagle in his eyrie, and the wolf from its covert, immediately upon the dying echoes a thousand braves shriek forth the savage sound, which, reverberating from rock to rock, amid the distant mountains, sounds like the very elements themselves were in discord.

At Fort Smith, we learned that Lyon and Siegel were pressing Price, who was retiring, before their superior numbers, toward the Arkansas line. Here the wagon-train was left, together with the sick men, disabled horses, etc., in command of Lieutenant Milburn, and the regiment, reduced to light marching order, hastened on to report to General Ben. McCulloch, the Confederate commander, whose headquarters were supposed to be somewhere near the Missouri line. Over the Boston mountains the command marched, the picturesque scenery of which extorted exclamations of admiration from all. Arkansas has been styled, with some degree of justness, the Scotland of America, and, perhaps, some future Scott shall spring up in the midst of that romantic landscape and recount, in epic numbers, the deeds enacted there when Titans grappled for the possession of the soil. Each day, nay, each hour, brought us tidings of the enemy's advance. That grand old Nestor of the Southern cause, Sterling Price, unable to stem the current of dark invasion, was leisurely retiring. As we neared the scene of operations, the demonstrations of welcome, on the part of the inhabitants, became more marked, until the town of Fayetteville was reached, where an enthusiastic ovation awaited us. Men, women, and children were transported with joy, and, amid the booming of "anvil" cannon, deafening cheers, and the waving of kerchiefs, wished us "God-speed."

The next night we encamped near Elk Horn tavern—a field

destined soon to become famous in the history of the war between the States. The headquarters of General McCulloch were reached about the 1st of August, on Cane Creek. The Missouri State Guard, commanded by General Price, had formed a junction with McCulloch's forces, and the two commanders were awaiting re-enforcements. The Missourians probably numbered 5,000 effective men. McCulloch's immediate command, consisting of the Third Louisiana Infantry and Third Texas Cavalry, did not exceed 2,000 men; and General Carroll, with about 2,000 Arkansas militia, completed the number of effective men under the Southern flag. All, save the Louisiana regiment, commanded by Colonel Louis Hebert, were poorly armed, the latter, having Mississippi rifles, were a well-uniformed, disciplined, and brave regiment. Thus, we ascertain, that the Confederate forces did not exceed 9,000 men, and they mostly raw recruits, with no drill instruction, and but little discipline. The enemy probably numbered 12,000 men, but this disparity in numbers is of but little moment when the greater disparity of arms, discipline, and munitions of war, generally, are taken into account. The enemy was largely composed of United States regulars, and his volunteer regiments, too, were armed with the latest and most improved weapons. The hostile armies were separated from each other by an interval of about five miles; upon which semi-neutral ground the Missouri cavalry was incessantly engaging that of the Federals in skirmishes and affairs of outposts. Here were seen, for the first time by our command, evidences of that vandalism which characterized the Federal soldiery throughout the war, and with which we were soon familiarized. A farm-house, deserted by its inmates at the Yankees' approach—which act proclaimed their Southern sympathies—had been occupied by the soldiers, and the most reckless waste and destruction indulged in, apparently, in a mere spirit of wanton deviltry. Here we filled our haversacks with three days' rations, and drew *ten rounds* of ammunition. When the EIGHTY rounds are remembered that we drew daily, and fired away, too, in the Atlanta campaign, this first year's soldiering seems like a "tempest in a tea-pot"—not that we didn't have warm work, for the brave and ill-fated Lyon struggled stubbornly for victory even when all hope had fled his cause. With the break of day, the advance commenced; the Missouri cavalry in front, the infantry in the center, and the Texas regiment on the left, or rear. All were in momentary expectation the "ball would open," but the wily Lyon, doubtful as to the numbers of McCulloch's recent re-enforcement, preferred to retire himself, and, by skillful maneuvering, compel the Confederate generals to discover their real strength. Since crossing the Missouri line, each man had acted as his own purveyor of supplies, and those supplies consisted almost exclusively of green corn, consequently, we were wolfish, and indulged in bright fancies of capturing the Federal army, bag and baggage (that always was the programme in those brave old days), and thereby bettering our commissariat.

Late in the afternoon of August 2, we encamped on the field destined to go down to the latest posterity as the "Battle-field of Oak Hills." Price's army occupied the road leading to Springfield; McCulloch's troops were encamped on, and adjacent to, Wilson Creek, about one and a half miles in the rear of Price. Lyon had retired to Springfield, which town he now occupied. For several days we remained in camp here. Scouting, skirmishing with the enemy's pickets, and procuring forage for man and beast, principally occupied the attention of the men. Captain Frank Taylor, of Company C, made a gallant dash into a detachment guarding a train loaded with supplies for Lyon, routing the detachment, taking a number of prisoners, and capturing the entire train.

On the afternoon of August 9, orders were issued to prepare three days' rations, clean up guns, and be prepared to advance on Springfield, at a moment's notice. The men hailed the order with acclamations of delight, but just about sun-setting, the order to march was countermanded, by reason of the threatening aspect of the heavens, and the men ordered to lie on their arms. This latter order extinguished the fires of enthusiasm, but, as the sequel proved, it was a precaution that saved the army. For, had we been negligently encamped, expecting no advance by the enemy, instead of achieving a victory, we must inevitably have been routed and captured, surrounded and surprised, as we were. And had we advanced upon Springfield, as originally intended, Price's column would have encountered Lyon's main force in the dark of the plutonian night, and been annihilated by it. The charge has been made, and denied, that the Confederate generals had no pickets stationed that night, in consequence of the expected advance. It does not seem possible that two officers, having the experience and reputation for prudence and caution that both Price and McCulloch enjoyed, would have thus left their commands to surprise. But if pickets were stationed, they were of no service, for the first intimation our regiment had that the enemy was near, was the report of Siegel's cannon and the whistling of shell just overhead.

Lyon and the Confederate commander had conceived the same plan of attack, and resolved to execute the same at about the same time, thus furnishing one of the most singular synchronisms that we ever remember having read of in this or any other war. In pursuance of this plan, Siegel was to turn the entire Confederate position, by taking a circuitous line of march, and open fire at daylight from his position immediately in our rear. Lyon was to advance in command of the main force, leisurely, not discovering his advance to Price until Siegel's signal-gun announced him in position. The entire plan of battle, so far, was carried out to the letter. Siegel formed in our rear, and his cannon boomed our reveille that morning. On our side, the surprise was complete. Price had intimation that the enemy was upon him a few moments before the artillery opened. Instantly, the command: "To horse!" was given, and the regiment marched out into an open field to await orders from General McCulloch. In passing a rail-fence, the second battalion of the regiment became cut off from the first, and took up position in column of fours near the scene of the late camp. Siegel, however, having changed his position by crossing the creek, now opened upon them a heavy fire of grape and canister. Being without a head, and having no orders to execute, Captain H. P. Mabry, a cool, brave, and determined officer, assumed command, and by a skillful movement, extricated the battalion from its unpleasant position.

By this time, the battle had become general. Lyon had opened upon Price along his entire line, and the Louisiana regiment and Arkansas infantry were engaging Siegel warmly. The rattle of musketry, and the thunder of artillery, were deafening. The hoarse shells groaned their solemn warning high in air, and the whistling minnieballs sounded many a poor fellow's requiem; while the shouts of the combatants rose often above the pandemonium of battle. The brave Louisianians would have routed Siegel alone, as they charged his left wing, driving it back in the utmost confusion. Not so the brave, but raw militia. The enemy—United States regulars—were pressing them heavily, and their line was beginning to waver, when General McCulloch rode up to Colonel Greer, and, in a few words, pointed out the state of affairs, and directed him to charge the advancing enemy. "Boys," shouted Colonel Greer, "remember you are Texans! Forward! trot! gallop! *charge!*" The enthusiastic shouts that greeted the latter order would have done justice to Cooper's Choctaw warriors. On! irresistibly on! the regiment swept. They were upon the Federals before a bayonet was fixed, and over the routed blue-coats it swept with the impetuosity of an alpine avalanche, as revolver and rifle dashed out many a life.

This sealed the fate of Siegel's command. They were routed and flying before the victorious Confederates, in all directions. Siegel, adopting the cry of the French at Waterloo: "Save himself who can!" succeeded in saving his bacon by the swiftness of his steed, and furnished a literal illustration of the truth of the doggerel:

> "He who fights and runs away,
> Will live to fight another day."

Siegel disposed of, General McCulloch hastened, with his entire command, to the assistance of General Price, who was hard pressed by his vigorous assailant. Captain H. P. Mabry, in command of a squadron, continued the pursuit of Siegel's broken and demoralized columns. Price and his brave Missourians had sustained the brunt of the battle, unaided, against greatly superior numbers. Charge after charge, the brave and determined Lyon made at the head of his columns, in person. Learning of Siegel's discomfiture, he fought with haste and impetuosity, but kept his men well in hand; and had he not fallen, the issue, possibly, might have been different. His fall was the signal for the shameful flight of his army, which deserted the dying hero-chieftain to the mercies of his triumphant, but magnanimous, enemy. They were unworthy of their leader; for, however much we may denounce the fanatical views of Lyon, and his intense hatred of every thing Southern, there is no question as to his being a strategist of the highest order of genius, and as brave and resolute to execute, as he was cool and sagacious to plan. He had maneuvered Price out of Missouri, and outgeneraled both Price and McCulloch, at the battle of Oak Hills. Had Siegel maintained his position with any credibility, Lyon could have put into execution other plans, which, doubtless, his fertile resources afforded him. But, as it was, he had no alternative but to strike as hard and rapidly as possible, thus reducing an excellently-planned battle, in which science should have performed a conspicuous part, to a mere brute contest. Though defeated, he displayed remarkable traits of character that stamped him as a master mind; and, had he lived, he certainly would have attained to eminence in the profession of arms. He sealed his convictions with his life's blood—falling within twenty steps of Price's line, where the missiles of death, like the Persian arrows at Thermopylæ, were so numerous as to obscure the light of the sun—and his foemen upon that well-contested field, willingly drop this pebble above his tomb.

As tending to further illustrate the subject, and, at the same time, present both sides of the question, as the readiest means of reconciling the discrepant statements of parties attached to different commands, on that memorable occasion, the annexed interview of T. L. Snead, Chief of Staff to General Price, with a correspondent of the Cincinnati *Enquirer*, is reproduced:

"Lyon," said Colonel Snead, "was the greatest man I ever knew. That has been my statement everywhere. I always felt it, and always said it. The day we had that memorable interview of six hours with him at the Planter's House, St. Louis, he was Jeff. Davis over again, but not as narrow and prejudiced as Davis. He was Davis, however, in intensity and tenacity, and about the leanness and height of Davis. We were to hold the interview in order to see if war could be prevented. I am the survivor of it. Claib Jackson and Sterling Price were the ablest politicians of Missouri; Price at the head after the death of Colonel Benton. I was the Governor's secretary. Lyon came there with Frank Blair, jr., and General Conant. Such was his force, clearness, and real genius, that he met these old politicians at every point, conceding nothing, but never discourteous, his reason and his will equal. The whole party felt him to be the master mind, and the Federal historians do not err when they put him down as the greatest general they produced—greater than any produced on both sides west of the Mississippi river. Lyon advanced into that room, a little, red-bearded, red-haired, precise, positive, plain man. He sat down, and crossed one leg over the other stiffly, and his face was serious and stern. He spoke each word separate from the other, pronouncing the little words, like *my* and *to*, with as much emphasis as the longer ones. He raised his right arm, automatically, as the conversation proceeded, and brought it down with a jerk, the forefinger extended, yet never speaking higher or lower than at first. We felt the sense of war and government in all his bearing. 'I shall take but a small part in this conference,' said Lyon; 'Mr. Blair is familiar with this question, and knows the views of my government, and has its full confidence; what he has to say will have my support.' Yet, in half an hour, he took the case out of Blair's mouth, and advanced to the front, and Frank Blair was as dumb as he had been. The United States could never have been typified by a more invincible mind and presence. It was three o'clock when the meeting broke up. The last attempt Jackson made, was to have both sides agree not to recruit troops in Missouri. Lyon arose: 'Rather than agree that my government shall concede to your government one iota of authority as to one man to be recruited, one inch of ground of this State to be divided in allegiance, or neutralized, between my government and your government, I will see all of us under the sod.' Then taking out his watch stiffly, he said: 'You shall have safe conduct out of my lines for one hour. Meantime, you can get your dinner.' It was now three o'clock. We took our dinner in haste, and left St. Louis by an express-train, and, if we had not burned the bridges behind us, he would have caught us before we reached Jefferson City, for he marched at once. Price had soldierly respect for him, and delivered up his body from the field of battle. It was found deserted a second time in the streets of Springfield. I then gave it to Mrs. Phelps, wife of the present Governor of Missouri, and sent men to bury it in the grave-yard at Springfield. Lyon followed us with a determination unparalleled in that war, and he went under the sod, in fulfillment of his vow." (Mr. Snead was Price's Adjutant-general at the time of the battle, as McIntosh, of Georgia, was McCulloch's.) "McIntosh was a better soldier than McCulloch, who was indecisive and faint of confidence. Price was a fine old officer, who had never lost a battle, and felt, like all Missourians, that the place to fight Lyon was in Missouri, and not to fall back to Arkansas. McCulloch commanded the Confederate army proper, of 3,000 men. Price commanded the Missouri State Guard of 8,000 men. The Confederate government, including Jeff. Davis, seemed indifferent about Missouri, and did not regard her as having properly seceded. Price was a Major-General—McCulloch only a Brigadier. The latter hesitated about marching upon Springfield, and was inclined to return to Arkansas. One day, Price rode up on his horse. He had a loud voice, and a positive address, and always spoke to McCulloch as if he considered the latter an inferior.

"'Do you mean to march into Missouri, and attack General Lyon, General McCulloch?'

"'I have not received permission from Mr. Davis to do so, sir,' answered McCulloch; 'my instructions leave me in doubt whether I would be justifiable in doing so.'

"'Now, sir,' said Price, still in a loud, imperious tone, 'I have commanded in more battles than you ever saw, General McCulloch; I have three times as many troops as you have; I am of higher rank than you are, and I am twenty years your senior in age. I waive all these things, General McCulloch, and, if you will march into Missouri, I will obey your orders, and give you the whole command, and all the glory to be won there.'

"McCulloch said he was then expecting a dispatch from Mr. Davis, and would take Price at his word, if it was favorable. The dispatch came, and the army advanced, with McCulloch in supreme command. After McCulloch had advanced awhile, he again grew irresolute, and, instead of moving on Springfield direct, he halted out at Wilson's Creek, twelve miles or so south of that city. Price rode up to him one day, and found him making diagrams on the ground with a stick. Price bawled out: General McCulloch, are you going to attack Lyon, or not?' McCulloch said that he was undecided. 'Then,' cried Price, 'I want my own Missouri troops, and I will lead them against Lyon, myself, if they are all killed in the action; and you, General McCulloch, may go where in the devil you please.' McCulloch was thus exasperated into promising an attack. It was arranged to move on the very night that Lyon moved, and by three columns, upon Springfield. In anticipation of this movement, McCulloch drew in his pickets, and, seeing some clouds and threatening weather arising, he ordered the troops to lay on their arms, and did not again advance his pickets. This led to the complete surprise effected by Lyon in the morning. At four o'clock, on the morning of the battle, August 10, 1861, McCulloch rode over to Price's headquarters, which were pitched in a sort of cow-yard, by a little farm-house down in a hollow.

While Price, McCulloch, Churchill, and Snead were taking breakfast at the earliest dawn, a man came in from the front, where Rains was posted, and said he had an important message. The Yankees were advancing full 30,000 strong, and were on Rains' line already. 'O, pshaw!' exclaimed McCulloch, 'that is only another of Rains' scares.' They then went on eating, until another man came and reported that the enemy was not more than a mile away, and right on Rains' column as they lay on their arms. McCulloch again said it was nonsense; but Price was excited. He thundered out to Snead: 'Order my troops, sir, under arms, and in line of battle at once, and have my horse saddled!' He had hardly spoken these words, when the little group of men looked up from the cow-yard to where the hills were rising, line on line, above them, and on the clear, morning perspective, they saw Totten's battery unlimbered on the top of a hill, less than three-quarters of a mile distant, and before he had thrown the first shot, Siegel's battery in the rear also pealed out, and the balls from those two cannon crossed each other right over the hollow in which Price's troops were lying. The surprise was perfect. General McCulloch hastened back to his headquarters, and put his troops in motion against Siegel. In a very little time, Siegel was whipped out. Price, in the meantime, had to encounter Lyon. The contest was spirited and deadly, and the weather like fighting in a furnace. Price's columns were reeling before Lyon's attacks, when he sent Colonel Snead to ask McCulloch if he could spare him a battalion of Missourians that were not properly in McCulloch's command. McCulloch then placed himself at the head of the Missouri column, with certain other troops, and came back over the field to Price's relief. It was this re-enforcement that caused the death of Lyon, as Colonel Snead believes; for, seeing fresh troops advancing on the Southern side, Lyon waved his sword, and led the counter-attack, and was shot dead. It was but a few minutes after Lyon fell before the battle ceased."

The foregoing is reproduced, in justice to the Missourians, for the reader must understand that there was foolish antagonism engendered between the troops of the rival generals, which was fanned into a blaze by a silly controversy conducted through the public journals of the land, by one Mr. Tucker, on the part of General Price, and by John Henry Brown, on the part of General McCulloch, which seriously impaired the efficiency of the army. But, in justice to "Ben

McCulloch"—name ever dear to every true Texan—we can not allow the charge of indecision to rest against the character of him who was decided in all things. His summary disposal of Siegel was the highest evidence of prompt decision. We would not detract one iota from the well-earned fame of Price and his noble Missourians, but it is but justice to place on record the fact that Ben. McCulloch displayed the high qualities of a commanding general on that occasion. He comprehended the situation at a glance, and decision came as if by intuition. He shared all the dangers of the field with the meanest of his men. But, as it will be more appropriate in a future chapter to dwell at length upon the character of General McCulloch, we will dismiss the subject until that time.

In Company A, Third Texas Calvary, was an unadulterated specimen from Erin, of the name of B. Thomas. Mr. Thomas rode an incorrigible horse, who would eat the tether that bound him to a tree, and, being loose, he would devour whatever was eatable in camp. This equine marauder had pursued his evil bent to such an extent, that many of the victims had become exasperated, and declared if Mr. Thomas did not devise means for securing the horse, they would kill him—the horse. As Mr. Thomas would have rather suffered crucifixion, head down, than to have been left afoot in Missouri, he procured a chain and padlock, with which he managed to secure the marauder. When Siegel's battery opened, just before dawn on that memorable morning, and the bugle rang out "to horse!" Mr. Thomas discovered that the mechanism of his lock was not perfect, for the "bloody thing would n't worruck." Siegel advanced, and the camp-ground became a battle-field. No one thought of Mr. Thomas until the command returned to camp in the evening, when lo! there stood the horse unscathed, and locked securely to a tree that had been literally peeled by the bullets. "Be the vargin!" exclaimed a husky voice from the dense bushes upon the creek; "boys, is the sthorm over till last?" It was Mr. Thomas, who had sought refuge in the bushes from the "inimy;" and, strange indeed, he had been as miraculously preserved as had the horse.

Another member of the same regiment was wounded in the charge upon Siegel's command, and left upon the field for dead. A party of Federal fugitives passing that way, robbed him of hat, boots, money. The ghouls felt his pulse and pronounced him dead, else he believes they would have administered the *coup de grace* with a bayonet. An original character, of the same regiment, was Mr. Brazil, who originally hailed from Buncombe county, Tar river, North Carolina. Mr. Brazil had a dozen ears of green corn on the fire when Siegel opened the matinee, which he swore he wouldn't leave for all the d——d Dutch in hell—for, be it known, that Lyon's army was composed so largely of Germans, that they were not called by the Confederates "Yanks," but "Dutch." When Mr. Brazil was satisfied the corn was cooked thoroughly, he took the dozen ears up in his arm, mounted his "war hoss," and with his old musket, as long as a fence-rail, lying in his lap, went jogging along in the direction he supposed the regiment had taken, while all his faculties were centered on an ear of corn upon which he was munching. "Hello! my man!" exclaimed an officer, as he rode up to one of Siegel's regiments, "Where are you bound, so early?" "O, by ——," exclaimed Brazil, with his mouth full of corn, "I'm gwine to ketch me a Dutchman, I am, you bet!" "Take him in, boys," fell upon the startled ears of the astonished Brazil, like the knell of doom. Mr. Brazil says they did "take him in," and "put him through," too, over a hundred miles of rocky road, at double-quick, afoot, to Rollo. The author certifies that Mr. Brazil, on his return to the command, was the worst used up man he ever saw. This episode gave Mr. Brazil a decided distaste to active operations in the field, and he became a teamster, and held the post unto the last. The love of lucre tempted him to substitute for another, after the expiration of his year's service; but he had it expressly stipulated that he was to retain his berth in the wagon-train.

When Siegel's shot began to fly pretty thick, brave, good old Captain Hale, who made no military pretensions, called out to his company: "Git in a straight row, here, boys! This is the war you all have hearn talked about! *Them's* the cannon; *them's* the muskets; that great big screeching thing is a bung-shell; and them little fellows that sing like bumble-bees, are minnie-balls! Git in a straight row; we're gwine to work, now!" And the brave old man and his gallant "boys" did good work on that memorable day.

The Third Texas Cavalry occupied the town of Springfield the day succeeding the battle, and the regimental flag was hoisted above the court-house, during which ceremony Major Chilton delivered an eloquent address to the assembled citizens and soldiers. Many Southern sympathizers, imprisoned merely for opinion's sake, were released from confinement in the county jail.

The body of the ill-fated Lyon was delivered to Mrs. Phelps, wife of the then member of Congress from the Springfield district, and at the present writing (1878), the Democratic Governor of Missouri, by whom it was interred on the premises of their homestead, two miles north of the town.

The author regrets that he can give no sketch of the life of the gallant, though unfortunate, Lyon.

The Federal loss in the engagement was severe—probably amounting to 1,000 killed, and twice that number prisoners and wounded. The Confederate loss did not exceed 250, all told. General McCulloch, after exchanging for the few Confederates in the hands of the enemy, dismissed the remainder of his prisoners, telling them that he had rather fight, than feed them.

The route of the Federal army was complete, and had the Confederate cavalry pursued, as the Prussians did at Waterloo, not a man would have reached St. Louis, which city—and it was the key to the West—must, undoubtedly, have been occupied by the Southern army. Unfortunately, there is recorded but few instances in which the Confederate soldier improved the advantages of victory. Had the enemy been pressed at Manassas and Oak Hills, Washington and St. Louis would have rewarded the efforts of the Confederates with bright promises of speedy and complete success. Secession, though it might have been a constitutional remedy, *i. e.*, in conformity to the *spirit* of the organic law, was a Cæsarian remedy, of so radical a nature as to be resorted to only in the extremest case. By abating no right under the Federal compact, the occupation of Washington would have been the possession of the government. The true policy, and only hope of the Confederacy, was in a spirited and aggressive warfare. Every thing should have been subordinated to efforts calculated to render the army efficient. One year should have ended the war; and it would have done so, could Southern statesmen have foregone the pleasure of splitting theoretical hairs, and came to the aid of the army with a tender of the resources of the whole country. The army performed its duty; the men performed prodigies of valor, and the officers were unsurpassed by any on the planet. But the crisis did not develop a single statesman capable of comprehending the magnitude of the struggle. Happily, now, these issues will arise no more to distract the American people from the high road to prosperity. If this Union is destined ever to be rent asunder, the entering wedge will not be applied by the South. This much is certain.

## BATTLE OF "OAK HILLS."

### I.

At midnight in the drear bivouac,
  The Southern patriots lay,
The storm-cloud with its somber black,
  Obscured the dismal way
Of the silent sentinel that kept
Lonely vigils while his comrades slept.

### II.

No camp-fire shed its dubious ray
  The spectral oaks to define,
Or light the stalwart forms that lay
  With rifles in battle line;
For, when the sun o'er the hill should glance,
McCulloch'd give the word to advance.

### III.

Reposing here, in fitful dream,
  Of home and loved ones far,
By old Wilson's turbid stream,
  The citizen-knights of war
Were eager to meet the foe in fight,
Beneath the "Bonnie Blue Flag," for right.

### IV.

Here waved Missouri's banner'd bear,
  Our lustrous "Lone Star" beside;
The tireless Pelican was there,
  Gay Louisiana's pride;
The tocsin Arkansas sounded, too,
And had mustered here her gallants true.

### V.

Morn at length from the dark night woke—
  A streak lit the eastern skies—
When the cannon of Siegel broke
  The silence with dire surprise,
Loud then the Federal thunder flew,
And louder the yell of triumph grew

### VI.

To arms, the banded heroes rushed,
   And formed their serried front,
With bated breath and lips still hushed,
   But eager to meet the brunt
Of battle, rushing with giant strides,
To humble Dixie's patriot pride.

### VII.

As leaps the angry tidal wave
   Upon the rock-ribbed shore,
So, when Lyon the order gave,
   The Regulars onward pour
Like mad billows from the dark blue sea,
For conquest sweeping the peaceful lea.

### VIII.

The shock of battle and the crush
   Of ranks, as wild squadrons wheel
And charge, with impetuous rush,
   The bright lines of deadly steel;
The cannon's hoarse and murderous roar—
The rifle's deadly rattle, and more—

### IX.

The saber's flash—the fatal thrust—
   The red wound, and ghastly death,
As iron hoofs tramp into dust
   The wounded, whose departing breath
Was nursed to give one parting cheer
For the cause the hero deem'd so dear.

### X.

In vain discipline sought to ride,
   In haughty victory o'er
Patriotism's devoted pride;
   Vain did the eagle lingering soar,
Above this human-created hell,
Which Siegel fled, and where Lyon fell.

### XI.

The pale, cold moon, her timid light,
   In dubious glances shed,
Over the beaten army's flight
   And over the silent dead
Of friend and foe, strewn thick around,
WHO WON, AND HELD, IN DEATH, THE GROUND.

# CHAPTER II.

ARRIVAL OF THE SIXTH TEXAS CAVALRY—INCIDENTS OF THE CAMPAIGN—MABRY AND JOHNSON'S GALLANT FIGHT—BIOGRAPHICAL SKETCH OF COLONEL GREER.

Captain Mabry pursued the routed and flying column of Siegel to a mill, situated on a creek some five miles from the field, capturing 150 prisoners. "And," says the MS. of Captain Dunn, "the road was thickly strewn with dead Federals." Siegel managed to retain possession of one piece of artillery up to this time, but, Mabry pressing him so close, he now consigned the whipped dog of war to the depths of the stream. No official account has been given to the public, so far as we know, of the losses sustained by the enemy in the battle. The fighting was at very close range, and the mortality immense. The dead and wounded literally encumbered the ground. With the exception of Mabry's pursuit, the enemy was allowed to seek safety in flight. An energetic pursuit by 1,000 cavalry would have bagged the whole fugitive mass; for never was defeat more thorough and demoralizing. The loss of the Texas regiment did not exceed ten killed and thirty wounded.

After the battle, the sad duty devolved upon the survivors to afford the wounded relief, and give to the dead the poor burial rights that they could. The duty of interring the enemy's killed also devolved upon the Confederate and Missouri soldiers, as the humane Siegel made no proposals to perform that obvious duty himself. Field hospitals were erected for temporary use, at the most convenient points, and the merciless surgical saw and knife commenced their work. The Southern forces occupied Springfield the next day, and to that town the wounded were speedily removed. The author, being one of the wounded, and in hospital, can certify that the excruciating sufferings of the poor fellows, exceeded the heart-rending scenes of the battle-field itself. Here reclines a poor Arkansian, in a half-sitting position, being supported by rolls of blankets, with a minnie-bullet through his bosom.  Each laborious respiration produces the fatal death rattle in his throat, and, though science knows the signet of death is fixed upon his clammy brow, the humane surgeons labor to alleviate his pain.  Gradually the breathing becomes less frequent, and the horrible gurgling rattle more weird and prolonged.  A silence ensues, and then a rustling from his distorted mouth, like the noiseless flapping of angel's wings which we hear, independent of the external sense, and the suffering soldier has passed from earth, with a smile of ineffable sweetness and confidence breaking upon his lips.  Did he, in passing the intermediate sphere, with one foot on the shores of Time, catch a glimpse of the cheering promise beyond?  None now may know.  Many other touching scenes might be added to this; but being in close proximity to the Arkansian, and an eye-witness of his death, the picture has remained stamped upon my mind as vividly as on that August day, in 1861.  General McCulloch, with that humanity characteristic of all noble natures, visited the hospitals in person, and had a cheering word for every sufferer.

The Missouri army commenced an immediate advance, and, to the deep chagrin and mortification of the Confederate army, we were suffered to remain in ignoble quietude, while our brave allies were winning new laurels at Lexington, and on other fields.  Whoever in authority was responsible for the fatal course that refused co-operation with General Price, was guilty of the most egregious folly capable of being committed by a man having the least pretension to reason and common sense.  Engaged in the same cause, Price's defeat would have been our loss, as his victories were our gain.  Yet we remained idle spectators, while the poorly-clad veterans of Missouri's "Old Guard" carried their "Grizzly Bears," from victory to victory, until overwhelming forces checked their splendid career; then, without sustaining a reverse, they sullenly retired, disputing every foot of ground with the giant enemy.  No brighter page will adorn the history of contemporary struggles, than the magnificent campaigns of these bare-footed boys, led by their grand old chieftain.  If heroism in the field, and Spartan fortitude in the midst of suffering and privations, had been acceptable sacrifices to the god of war, the rich libation of their blood would have invoked, successfully, the genius of victory to perch upon their banners.  But so it was not decreed in the chancery of Heaven.

General McCulloch's forces remained encamped in the south-western portion of Missouri, doing little else than cooking and eating the wholesome and abundant rations furnished them by the commissariat, until Fremont's vain-glorious advance to Springfield, driving Price before him, when the Confederate army retired to the "Cross Hollows," seemingly a favorite position of General McCulloch. But as the Sixth Texas Cavalry joined us previous to this time, we will now take a brief review of its organization, regretting that the meager *data* available renders it impossible to go more into details. For the Sixth deserves the highest eulogium that can be pronounced in its praise. Composed, like the other regiments that early left the State, of the very best young men in the country, it could be relied upon to accomplish any feat of daring within the prowess of human bravery and daring.

In August, 1861, Colonel B. Warren Stone, of Dallas, was commissioned a Colonel, by the President of the Provisional Government, and immediately issued a call, inviting the formation of companies. On the 6th of September following, the subjoined companies were organized as the Sixth Regiment of Texas Cavalry, and were mustered into the service of the Confederate States, at Camp Bartow, in Dallas county, by Colonel Garland:

Co. A, Kaufman county, —— Harden, Captain.
Co. B, Kaufman county, John S. Griffith, Captain.
Co. C, Dallas county, Fayette Smith, Captain.
Co. D, Grayson county, —— Bowen, Captain.
Co. E, Van Zant county, Jack Wharton, Captain.
Co. F, Dallas county, —— Gray, Captain.
Co. G, McLennan county, P. F. Ross, Captain.
Co. H, Bell county, —— White, Captain.
Co. I, Henderson county, H. W. Burgess, Captain.
Co. K, Collin county, J. W. Throckmorton, Captain.

Each company averaged something over 100 men; the regiment aggregating 1,150. An election of field officers was immediately held, the Colonel also submitting his name for the approval of his men. The election resulted as follows:

B. Warren Stone, of Dallas county, Colonel.
John Summerfield Griffith, Lieutenant-Colonel.

Private L. S. Ross, of Company G, was elected Major.
Lieutenant D. R. Gurley, of Company G, was appointed Adjutant.
Captain A. J. White, of Dallas, Quartermaster.
Captain ——— —————, of Collin county, Commissary of Subsistence.

The regiment soon moved up to Collin county, and encamped near McKinney, and while in camp at this place, was reviewed by Colonel Garland. The regiment, being well mounted and well clad, presented a fine appearance, upon which they were handsomely complimented by Colonel Garland. The "sound of resounding arms" had fallen on their ears, and the boys were eager impatience itself to get to the front, and bear a hand in the efforts of Mr. Abraham Lincoln to make history. After a few days' stay at McKinney, the regiment took up the line of march for Missouri, being, for the convenience of obtaining forage, divided into three divisions, of which Major Ross commanded the first, Lieutenant-Colonel Griffith the second, and Colonel Stone the third. This order of march was continued until Red river was crossed, when the various divisions were consolidated again at Northtown. At this point, information reached Colonel Stone that a large body of hostile Indians were driving the command of Colonel Cooper back. The regiment immediately commenced a forced march in the direction of Fort Gibson. Having reached this place, the news was more definite and confirmatory of the reports before received. Hopotheohola, a veteran chief, who had fought with the hostiles at Talladega and Horse Shoe, had gathered together the disaffected of all the tribes, and, under the designation of "Pin Indians," had taken the field in sufficient numbers as to compel the Confederate Indian Superintendent, Colonel Cooper, to retire before him. From Fort Gibson, the regiment continued the forced march up the Verdigris. But the wily old chief, hearing of Cooper's anticipated re-enforcement, turned about and retreated in the direction of Kansas, burning and laying waste the country along his route. Hopeless of overtaking the hostiles, as his horses were already much jaded, Colonel Stone countermarched and returned to Fort Gibson. From here the regiment proceeded leisurely to Camp Walker, in Missouri, where were pitched the headquarters of General McCulloch. After reporting to General McCulloch, the regiment then proceeded to Carthage, where General

McCulloch was concentrating his cavalry, preparatory to making a raid into Kansas.

On September 28th, the patriot Governor of Missouri, Claiborne F. Jackson, who, like the rejected Son of Man, literally, had not where to lay his head within the broad domain of the Commonwealth over which he was titular Chief Magistrate, with his staff and escort, approached Carthage. Colonel Greer proceeded, at the head of his regiment, to do the honors of the day to the almost fugitive Governor, and escort him into town. The Governor reviewed the regiment, and took up his quarters in the town. On the night of the 30th, he delivered an eloquent defence of the secession of Missouri, to a large concourse of citizens and soldiers. Standing upon the steps of the court-house, his silvery hair reflecting the mellow beams of moonlight, he presented a picture of Justice wronged, and the impotency of Virtue, alone, to cope with the minions of Might and Wrong. In this address, Governor Jackson imparted to us the first intimation of the proposed invasion of Kansas. In speaking of the enormities perpetrated by the ruthless Kansas "Jayhawkers," upon the defenseless citizens of the border counties of Missouri, he raised his trembling hand aloft and exclaimed: "In ten days, we will turn upon them the most ruthless invasion known to man since the razing of Jerusalem to the earth, and burn the accursed land from Dan to Beersheba!" This retaliatory programme, it is supposed, would have been carried out, had not the intelligence reached General McCulloch, at that time, of General Price's retreat from Missouri, closely followed by General Fremont. This General, it is said, assumed the consequence of an eastern satrap, and so encumbered was he with the immense wagon-train necessary to transport the delicacies of his luxurious camp, that he made but a desultory pursuit of General Price, and, like the dog in pursuit of the wolf, was not extremely anxious to overtake him. The short march, from St. Louis to Springfield, proved enough *active* campaigning for General Fremont, and, in the latter town, he established his court, and remained until the commencement of the winter season in St. Louis, when he removed his court to the gay capital of his satrapy. Hearing of Fremont's departure, General McCulloch hastily placed himself at the head of a cavalry force, of which our Texas regiments and Whitfield's Battalion formed an integral part, and made a rapid march to Springfield, only to find that General Fremont, having rusticated sufficiently, had leisurely returned to St. Louis.

While Fremont was encamped at Springfield, General McCulloch ordered Captain Mabry with his company G, and Captain Cumby with company B, both of the Third Texas, to proceed to Springfield, or as near that town as they could, without risking too much the capture of their commands, and to ascertain approximately the number of the enemy, the number of his guns, and all other information concerning him they could obtain. When within about ten miles of Springfield, these brave officers were met by a regiment of Missouri cavalry that had been skirmishing with the enemy's pickets, the commander of which informed them that Fremont occupied the place with 50,000 men, and that they had better turn back, as their capture would be certain, if they proceeded any further in that direction. But these brave and conscientious officers did not think they had fulfilled the spirit of their instructions, and resolved to pursue their present course and risk the consequences. They proceeded to within eight miles of the town, and ascertained of a Southern sympathizer, at whose house they had halted to make inquiries, that the enemy was full 35,000 strong, and that his forces were encamped immediately within the limits of the town. It was judged inadvisable to proceed any further with the men; and, at the suggestion of the dauntless Mabry, Cumby remained in charge of the two companies, and himself, accompanied by Captain Alf. Johnson and a thoroughly reliable guide, set out, determined to obtain the information desired by General McCulloch. They proceeded without incident to within one mile of Springfield, and here fastening their horses, entered the town afoot, and made for the house of a well-known Southern lady. From her they learned that the enemy was reported to be 30,000 strong. Dispatching the guide for a Southern gentleman, from whom the desired information could be obtained, Mabry and Johnson proceeded to regale themselves with a warm supper that had been prepared for them. After supper, Mabry went out into the front yard to ascertain if all was right, and his quick eye immediately discovered the fact that the house was surrounded by Yankees. Turning to re-enter the house, he was accosted by a party of five or six, who demanded his surrender and the yielding up of his arms. Pretending to comply, the dauntless man drew his bowie knife and plunged it into the heart of the spokesman, who dropped dead at his feet. This was the signal for a terific onslaught. The infuriated Yankees closed in on him, while revolver after revolver rung out its murderous report. Mabry slashed right and left in the darkness with his trusty knife, and other foemen, undoubtedly, felt the keenness of its edge. But he is now shot through the right hand and the friendly knife drops from his nerveless grasp at his feet. Drawing his revolver with his left hand, he retreats around the house to where Johnson is engaged with a number of the enemy; for, upon the first report of fire-arms, Johnson jumped out of the window, and was met by a number of men, who demanded his surrender. His only reply was from the muzzle of his shot-gun. Emptying both barrels of which, he, too, drew his six-shooter and continued the bloody fray. Mabry having rejoined him, the two kept the enemy at bay as they retired from the scene, Johnson supporting himself upon the shoulder of Mabry, as he was severely wounded in the hip. The indomitable men proceeded thus until they reached their horses, when they made for Captain Cumby and the two companies. The faithful guide, hearing the uproar, immediately retraced his steps, and procuring their overcoats, letters, etc., rejoined them at camp. Take this episode in all its bearing, and, I suppose, it stands unparalleled in all the hairbreadth escapes of the war for cool courage and indomitable will. Julius Cæsar was no braver than H. P. Mabry, and the writer has often thought that, if Mabry had commanded at Vicksburg, there would have been no surrender of that place, and, *ergo*, no necessity for the sad finale at Appomattox Court-house. After reaching the command, the two wounded heroes had time and leisure to realize how hazardous had been their mission, and how narrow their escape. Their clothing was literally perforated by the enemy's balls, and it seemed that the hand of death had been averted only by a miracle. Of Captain Mabry's subsequent career, our narrative will deal. Captain Johnson was afterwards appointed to a Colonelcy, for his gallantry on this occasion, and was the commandant of Arkansas Post, when that place fell into the hands of the enemy. He was taken prisoner and died in St. Louis. After the reconnoissance, at Springfield, General McCulloch retired toward the Arkansas line, and, about December 6, 1861, the various regiments went into winter-quarters.

The winter encampment of the Third was selected at the mouth of Frog bayou, on the Arkansas river, and that of the Sixth a few miles below. Captain Harris, the energetic Quartermaster of the Third, procured a saw-mill, and soon material for the erection of comfortable shanties, was in abundance. As there were no rumors of war here, the boys commenced a life of pleasure and social dissipation in the fashionable circles of Frog bayou. Dances—regular old-fashioned "bran-dances"—were the order of the night; and animated jig and reel followed the lively twanging of many an Arkansaw Ole Bull's fiddle. Many of the boys here obtained furloughs for the purpose of visiting their homes. General McCulloch went to Richmond, Virginia, the permanent capital of the Confederacy, and Colonel Greer obtained leave of absence to visit his home, which left the army in command of General McIntosh, and the regiment in command of Lieutenant-Colonel Lane.

# CHAPTER III.

### DEATH OF CAPTAIN HARRIS—BATTLE OF CHUSTENAHLAH—WINTER-QUARTERS—KINDNESS OF MRS. GREER, ETC.

Early in December, the Third Regiment was called upon to mourn the loss of their good old quartermaster. In superintending the sawing of timber, Captain Harris carelessly allowed his clothing to be caught by the teeth of the circular saw, and, ere the team could be stopped, his body was fearfully mangled. He survived a day or two, and died. No regiment in the service had the good fortune to possess a better quartermaster than he, and his loss was long and seriously felt by the men.

The festivities alluded to in the preceding chapter were at their height—like the celebrated ball at Brussels, immortalized by Byron—when the rude blast of war broke upon the diverting scene, and summoned the gay Adonis from blushing sweetheart and nimble-toed jig, to ruder scenes in the march, the bivouac, and the deadly charge. The irrepressible Hopotheohola, daring the rigors of winter as he had braved the frosts of time, had again flung his seditious standard to the breeze, and defiantly thrown down the gage of battle to General Cooper, who immediately commenced a periodical retreat. Simultaneously with the reception of the intelligence, Colonel McIntosh ordered out the cavalry, consisting of the Third, Sixth, and Eleventh (Young's) Texas Regiment, and Whitfield's Battalion (Texas), the latter two of whom had but recently joined us. Placing himself at the head of the column, McIntosh gave the signal for the march to commence. At Van Buren, where the command crossed the Arkansas river, McIntosh's regiment of mounted infantry fell into line. A forced march was here begun, which terminated only when Fort Gibson was reached. The weather, previously very pleasant, now became extremely cold. The ground was frozen, and the men suffered much from the bitter cold. Passing through Fort Gibson, the command crossed a large prairie, and entered the woods beyond, through which flowed the Chustenahlah creek, a beautiful and wild mountain brook. From this point, the smoke from the enemy's camp-fires was plainly visible, rising from the summits of the mountains in the distant perspective. The command halted on Chustenahlah creek until midnight, when Colonel Lane, throwing forward Company E (Third Regiment), Captain D. M. Short commanding, as an advance-guard, the command resumed the line of march. The march was continued all night without an incident to vary the dull monotony. About 9 P.M., Captain Short came upon the enemy's pickets, and drove them rapidly in upon the main body. The command soon arrived upon the scene, when it was discovered that the enemy was posted upon the summit of an almost inaccessible mountain. The sagacious and experienced Hopotheohola had selected a position impregnable by nature, and the veteran chieftain, with his more youthful lieutenant—Halleck Tschustenuga—were riding up and down the lines, speaking words of confidence, and imparting hopes of promise, in an effort to rouse their warriors to as sublime a devotion to the cause, and reckless disregard of consequences, as filled their own stoical bosoms. The warriors, painted in the most hideous manner, and clad in the most outlandish garbs, were perpetrating fantastic antics before high heaven, and the cat-like enemy ready for the fatal spring below. Some gobbled, in imitation of the turkey-gobbler; others, fired by a spirit of emulation, apparently, rivaled the coyote in howling; the game viking of the barn-yard would have recognized his "cock-a-doodle-doo," in the wild pandemonium of sounds, as would the panther, the catamount, and even the domestic dog.

Colonel McIntosh determined to charge the almost perpendicular mountain, on horseback. Upon the side next us there was but little timber to afford us shelter from the unerring marksmen covered by their works, but there were large, craggy rocks to be scaled, and bottomless gulches to be passed. The command was immediately deployed into line. The Sixth, commanded by Lieutenant-Colonel John S. Griffith, on the right; the Third, commanded by Lieutenant-Colonel Lane, in the center; the Eleventh, commanded by Colonel Wm. C. Young, on the left; McIntosh's battalion of infantry supporting the line. Slowly the command marches to the very base of the last elevation, and the enemy's sharpshooters are commencing to fire. But the impetuous McIntosh, who can not brook a tardy skirmish salutation, orders the charge, and the intrepid Lane and Griffith, responding, call on their men, and a thousand frenzied yells reply, as a thousand excited horses plunge madly up the steep ascent, and a thousand rifles pour such a leaden hail into the ranks of the astounded and terrified Indians, that no effort is made to hold the works, and the victory is won ere the battle had fairly begun.

A vigorous pursuit was immediately commenced, and many hand-to-hand fights to the death occurred; for, however impotent the Indian may be *fettered* by disciplined organization, individually, he knows no personal danger, and, taking his life in his hand, will accept the challenge to mortal combat with the odds against him of ten to one. The Indians scattered in all directions—having Kansas, however, for the objective point—and built fires, or rather made "smokes," in order to divert the pursuers, and cause them to relax the pursuit. One instance of their stoical indifference to death will suffice: An old warrior fired upon a party of eight or ten from behind a tree. The men did not wish to kill him, and used even entreaties to induce him to surrender; but, with death imminent, he continued to load his old rifle with a sublime indifference never attained by the Cynic philosophers of Greece, and, having loaded, he coolly proceeded with the priming, when his admiring foes were compelled to dash out his brave old life. "Only an Indian killed!" but who knows what the hopes were that this old man had founded upon his cause? Go, votaries of the "Lost Cause," to the crumbling stones of your dismantled altars, and invoke, if ye can, the spirit of 1861. It is dead! dead in soul and body, and no wraith even represents it in the phantom processions of the shadowy land of Weir! The victors at Atlanta and Appomattox hold it even lighter than you regard the cause of the poor old warrior, lying there in the silent wilderness before you, with his crimson life-tide ebbing and splashing away! Unhappy man, in the brief span of life, is but a puppet! The Roman emperor weighs not more in the balances of Divine justice than does the savage Indian; each leaves the impress of his foot upon the sands of time, and the first returning wave obliterates all trace of empire and tribe alike.

An inventory of the captured prisoners and property showed: Two hundred and fifty women and children; forty or fifty negroes; five hundred head of ponies; seventy or eighty wagons; one hundred head of beef cattle; five hundred head of sheep; ten thousand (more or less) dogs; besides buffalo-robes, beads, belts, and other trinkets too numerous and infinitesimal to name. One article found among the trinkets, invaluable by reason of its age and antecedents, was a silver medal, struck in commemoration of a treaty of peace concluded between the Creeks and the British Government, in the year 1694. What became of this souvenir, the author knows not; but hopes it has been returned, ere this, to its original owners.

The loss of the command was slight, but no correct list, it is thought, of the casualties, is now extant. Lieutenant Durham, a young and promising officer of Company B, Third Regiment, was mortally wounded, and died soon after. Company A, of the Third Regiment, was ably commanded by Orderly-Sergeant R. B. Gause, whose many noble qualities deserve that he should be mentioned; but the author knows no eulogium that he could pronounce in his praise more appropriate than that pronounced by the great Napoleon on Baron Larry: "He was," said the Emperor, "the most virtuous man I ever knew."

That the United States had stirred up this revolt among the Indians, the United States rifles with which they were largely armed, amply demonstrated. But the emissaries of the Federal Government were powerless again to cause the Indian to offer himself as food for powder and lead. The crushing defeat of Chustenahlah put a period to all hopes of creating a diversion in that direction. Poor old Hopotheohola, who had done all that individual sagacity and intrepidity could, with the limited means at his command, fell a victim to his discomfited warriors' desire for revenge and blood. He was assassinated by unknown parties soon after the battle. The campaign proper terminated with the battle of Chustenahlah, and the command of Colonel McIntosh returned to their respective quarters. In the case of the Third Regiment, the boys were glad enough to return to their comfortable quarters, and resume the social duties and pleasures that had been so unceremoniously broken up by the late call to arms. Colonel Greer, soon after this, returned, being accompanied by his charming and good lady. We have spoken elsewhere of the angelic ministrations of Mrs. Greer, at the bedside of the sick soldiers, and would again repeat all that we there wrote; and did the language admit of more positive expressions, they should be employed in commendation of her Christian deeds.

About the latter portion of February, the men who had been home on furlough reported for duty, and many fresh volunteers came, also, to swell the ranks of the regiment. Of course, these neophytes in the art of war looked upon their veteran friends of twelve months' service as perambulating military encyclopedias of useful knowledge. The veteran felt his importance, and, oracle-like, delivered his replies to the many questions by metaphorical allusions, and with an air of freezing indifference. A new recruit, upon one occasion, desired to be informed, by a veteran friend, how many Yankees he had killed. The impossibility of ascertaining this fact, in a general engagement, was shown by the veteran. " Did you ever kill *one?*" persisted the recruit. "Did you ever shoot one, and see the blood spout out—see it, yourself?" "It is better," replied the veteran, "to be in doubt whether we ever killed *one*, than to have the conscience tormented with the belief that we killed them all." This was satisfactory.

While in winter-quarters, as Adjutant M. D. Ector was attempting to suppress some boisterous noise in the camp of one of the companies, he was assaulted by two of the men, who were subsequently court-martialed, and sentenced to be dishonorably discharged and drummed out of the regiment. The sentence was severe, and the unfortunate men, who had proved themselves good and brave soldiers, felt the disgrace deeply.

The negroes, and a portion of the women and children captured at Chustenahlah, were kept under guard at this post for several weeks. What ultimately was the fate of the poor unfortunates, we know not. They presented a forlorn and pitiful picture—bereft of all they held dear—and the author's heart, on more than one occasion, went out in sympathy to them.

### INCIDENTS, ETC.

On the evening of the 25th, as the Third Texas was busy in the work of pitching camp, two hundred warriors, as if they had emerged from the bosom of the earth, were discovered in line of battle, not exceeding one-half mile, in the immediate front of the regiment, calmly contemplating the actions of the busy and unconscious men before them. Major Chilton rode out about halfway toward them, and signified, by signs, for one to approach him, which request was immediately complied with. The Indians refused to speak the American language, by which token Major Chilton was soon convinced that they were hostiles, and abandoned the conference; whereupon, the silent cavalcade as mysteriously disappeared in the mountains as it had appeared. Just before night, on this evening, Sam. Martin, an old Indian fighter, discerned the smoke of the hostile encampment rising above the summits of the mountains, in the dim distance, and forthwith reported the fact to Colonel Lane, and from this moment, all fears of the enemy's retreat were dispelled.

Hopotheohola had, at one time, exercised the functions of Chief of the Creek Nation, and was displaced by the able and favorite "White King," McIntosh, who was succeeded by his son, Chili, who, as chief, concluded a treaty with General Pike, on the part of the Confederate States, in 1861. A bitter feud existed between Hopotheohola and the McIntosh family, and for Chili McIntosh to espouse the cause of the South, was sufficient reason why his hereditary enemy should cast his fortunes on the opposite side. The full-bloods generally sided with Hopotheohola, while the wealth and intelligence of the tribe arrayed themselves under the banner of the legitimate chief, McIntosh, who proved himself an able leader, a sagacious ruler, and a man of unswerving fidelity to the cause he had espoused. Indeed, there were instances in which the civilized Indians signalized themselves for high courage, fortitude, and chivalry, that would have reflected credit on knights of the "Round-Table;" conspicuous among whom must always stand the names of Chili McIntosh and Colonel Stan Waitie.

Colonel McIntosh's plan of campaign comprised the capture of the enemy as well as his defeat; and, to this end, Colonel D. H. Cooper, commanding an Indian brigade, to which was temporarily attached the Ninth Regiment of Texas Cavalry, and Whitfield's Texas Battalion—both of which organizations, subsequently, were integral parts of "Ross' Brigade"—marched up the Arkansas river with the object of cutting off the retreat of the enemy, while the command of Colonel McIntosh, as before stated, marched up the Verdigris, and attacked Hopotheohola on the heights of Chustenahlah. The immediate object of the movement was defeated by the precipitancy of the attack, and the immediate giving way of the Indian line. But the indefatigable Whitfield, the gallant Colonel Sims of the Ninth, and Colonel Cooper, with his brigade of friendly Indians, pursued them far into the inhospitable plains. The pursuers were forced to turn back, as their rations were consumed, and they had already tested the quality of broiled horse-flesh. The plains were utterly destitute of game. The weather was intensely cold, and, in addition to the pangs of hunger, the men suffered no little from this cause.

Major G. W. Chilton, of the Third Texas Cavalry, while acting with conspicuous gallantry, was wounded by a rifle-ball, slightly, in the head; but, disregarding which, he remained at his post until the last gun was fired. Major M. J. Brinson, of the Ninth Texas Cavalry, bore himself, throughout the engagement, with marked gallantry; and, by his fearless demeanor, contributed no little to the final result. The author's friend, Harry Bell, of Company A, Third Texas Cavalry, was severely, though not mortally, wounded by a frightful bullet-hole in the right breast.

At Fort Gibson, Lieutenant-Colonel Lane obtained leave of absence, and returned home, leaving Major G. W. Chilton in command of the Third Texas Cavalry, which leisurely continued the march to winter-quarters. At Van Buren, Major Chilton munificently "stood treat," and purchased a barrel of choice whisky, which the boys of the regiment disposed of by drinking frequent "potations pottle deep," and all got as merry as merry could be, and many did n't get home till morning, and some, only after the lapse of two or three days; but, in the case of these latter, whether their absence was attributable to the effects of Arkansaw corn-juice, or to Arkansaw belles, deponent sayeth not.

One of the unostentatious heroes of Chustenahlah, was B. S. Triplett, the author's friend, and to whom he was indebted for many an act of kindness. Brave and loyal "old Tripp," after passing through the hundreds of battles and skirmishes of the four years of war, fell just at its close by the hands of an assassin. Perhaps it was better so! He never lived to look upon the "conquered banner," and to feel that experience of death in life that he had outlived his usefulness. Death is generally accounted the ultimate loss; but death often relieves life of many burdens too grievous to be borne; and, it is doubtful, if we should not look upon the white horse and his specter rider as friends of humanity, instead of remorseless foes.

## ORGANIZATION, AND FIRST YEAR'S SERVICE OF THE NINTH TEXAS CAVALRY.

To its gallant and noble Colonel, W. B. Sims, now a leading merchant of Jefferson, Texas, the author is indebted for the data from which is evolved the subjoined brief reference to the organization of the Ninth Texas Cavalry, and its services up to the first day's fight at Elk Horn, on March 6, 1862. The regiment was originally organized for State service, at Brogden's Springs, about twelve miles north of Sherman, Grayson county, October 2, 1861, with the following officers:

    Colonel—W. B. Sims, Red River county.
    Lieutenant-Colonel— ——— Quail, Tarrant county.
    Major—N. C. Towns, Red River county.
    Surgeon— ——— Robinson, Titus county.
    Assistant Surgeon— ——— Prewitt, Titus county.
    Adjutant—Dudley Jones, Titus county.

(D. W. Jones was elected Colonel at the re-organization of the regiment at Corinth, Mississippi, in May, 1862.)

    Quartermaster—W. B. Sims, Red River county.
    Commissary—J. D. Wright, Lamar county.
    Co. A, Tarrant county, Thos. G. Berry, Captain.
    Co. B, Fannin county, Sid. Smith, Captain.
    Co. C, Grayson county, J. E. McCoole, Captain.
    Co. D, Tarrant county, M. J. Brinson, Captain.
    Co. E, Red River county, J. C. Hart, Captain.
    Co. F, Titus county, W. E. Duncan, Captain.
    Co. G, Hopkins county, L. D. King, Captain.
    Co. H, J. D. Wright, Captain, who was appointed Commissary of Subsistence at Horsehead, and E. L. Dohoney was elected Captain.
    Co. I, Titus county, Chas. S. Stewart, Captain.
    Co. K, Hopkins county, J. P. Williams, Captain.

The regiment was mustered into the Confederate States' service October 14, 1861, by Colonel W. C. Young; and, in a very short while, Colonel Sims received orders to report, with his command, to General Ben. McCulloch, whose headquarters were located in South-west Missouri. *En route*, in conformity to these instructions, Colonel Sims received, at North Forktown, in the Indian Territory, orders from General McCulloch directing him to proceed to the assistance of General D. H. Cooper, who was being pressed by a superior force of hostile Indians. In compliance with this order, the command was turned, and soon Colonel Sims received an urgent appeal from General Cooper to the effect that he should forward five hundred men, in charge of Lieutenant-Colonel Quail and Major Towns, by forced marches, to his assistance. Volunteers were called for, and, the whole regiment responding, Colonel Sims caused the requisite number to be detailed, when the march was immediately commenced. Arriving at General Cooper's quarters, Lieutenant-Colonel Quail was directed to have his men cook seven days' rations, and otherwise prepare for assuming the offensive. The night was spent in making the necessary preparations, and, with the early dawn, the march was resumed. Hopotheohola, a veteran ex-chief of the Creeks, was in command of the hostiles. These burned the grass, and destroyed every thing eatable, in the line of the Confederate advance; and, as the boys were novices in campaigning, and knew not the necessity of economizing their rations, the consequence was that the supply was soon exhausted.

On the fourth day out, the village of Hopotheohola was sighted, and Lieutenant-Colonel Quail immediately made dispositions for battle. This was on November 19. The regiment was divided; a portion in charge of Lieutenant-Colonel Quail, deflecting to the right, in the edge of the timber, and the remainder, under Major Towns, obliqueing to the left through the prairie. In a short time, Lieutenant-Colonel Quail came upon the enemy, and attacked him vigorously. This battle was quite stubbornly contested by Hopotheohola, but Colonel Quail finally drove them from the field, and won the victory of Round Mountain. Captain Stewart, of Titus county, was killed while gallantly leading his men, and several of the men were killed and wounded. The Indians fired the grass in such a manner as to throw the glare upon the whites, while the shadow of the dense smoke afforded them a friendly cover. The command camped upon the field with horses saddled and arms in hand, and, in the early dawn, set out upon the trail of the retreating foe. Several of the Texans had been taken prisoners at Round Mountain, and were tortured and killed by the savages on their retreat. Their mutilated bodies—always scalped—were properly interred by their comrades.

On December 9, another engagement was had with Hopotheohola, on Bird's creek, in which Colonel Sims again defeated him, with but slight loss on the part of the whites. The battle was spirited, and continued for the space of three hours. The next day, Colonel Sims received orders to report at Fort Gibson, and to assume command of that post until further orders. The Ninth remained at this place until the arrival of Colonel McIntosh, when the Chustenahlah campaign was inaugurated, as elsewhere recounted in these pages. The fugitives from that fatal field were pursued by the regiment of Colonel Sims, the battalion of Major Whitfield, and the Indians of General Cooper's immediate command, far into the bleak and inhospitable plains of Kansas, whose death-brooding alkali soil nourished nothing for the subsistence of man or horse. The men, in consequence, suffered no little from the pangs of hunger and cold, and were forced, finally, to the alternative of starving outright, or eating "mule-beef."

On returning to Fort Gibson, Colonel Sims was ordered to proceed to Van Buren, Arkansas, and from there the regiment marched to Horsehead bayou and went into winter-quarters. The men had, however, scarcely completed their cabins, and were beginning to feel comfortable, when the regiment was ordered to report to General McCulloch, at Fayetteville. This was the opening of the campaign that terminated in the drawn battle of Elk Horn, or Pea Ridge, as the Union historians have named it. Colonel Sims opened the fight, on the part of McCulloch's corps, by a splendid charge upon a Federal battery, which he captured, with the loss of about twenty men and twice that number of horses. The gallant Sims, while intrepidly leading his men in the charge, had his right arm broken by a grape-shot, and was forced, reluctantly, to quit the field. In about the space of one hour from this time, Colonel Sims received the intelligence of General McCulloch's fall, and immediately dispatched his ambulance for the body of the General. This he conveyed to Bentonville, Arkansas, and delivered it into the charge of Major Brown, of McCulloch's staff.

After the battle, the regiment leisurely fell back to Van Buren, at which place it remained several days, and until orders were received for dismounting of the men, and their transfer to the Cis-Mississippi department. The regiment embarked for Memphis, Tennessee, at Des Arc, April 16, 1862, and were soon transported by rail to Corinth, where they were brigaded with the Sixth Texas, and other regiments which constituted Phifer's Brigade, of Maury's Division. Of their subsequent services, the narrative speaks in connection with those of the other regiments which constituted the "Texas Brigade," which was first commanded by Brigadier-General J. W. Whitfield, and, subsequently, by General L. S. Ross.

The NINTH was a splendid body of young men, who signalized their valor and devotion to the cause of their section on many of the bloodiest fields of the war.

## CHAPTER IV.

VAN DORN ARRIVES AND ASSUMES COMMAND—ELK HORN—DEATH OF McCULLOCH AND McINTOSH—INCIDENTS, ETC.

The peaceful, semi-domestic scenes that characterized the sojourn in winter-quarters, were of short duration, for soon the summons came for us to mount and go forth, to meet a more powerful foe than the one so recently vanquished on the heights of Chustenahlah. The heroic Price had made a winter campaign into Missouri, and the "Old Guard" had added fresh laurels to their fame by the victory of Drywood, and on other fields. About the middle of February, General Curtis took the field, at the head of about 40,000 men, magnificently equipped, and abundantly provided with all the murderous machinery of war. Price had halted at Springfield, purposing to spend the remainder of the winter there, in the re-organization of his army. In an address to the people of Missouri, he eloquently exclaimed: "Give me 50,000 men, and Missouri shall march to victory with the tread of a giant!" At Carthage, in the autumn past, a quorum of the Missouri Legislature had convened, and formally severed her connection with the United States, and, in conformity to this "Act," General Price was mustering the State Guard into the Confederate service; and, in the midst of his labors, he was apprised of the enemy's advance. The brave old man did not move until the enemy was upon him. Then, placing his raw recruits in front, with the immense wagon-train, that he had filled with supplies from the fertile fields of Missouri, he commenced his slow and stubborn retreat. And woe to the enemy's column that had the temerity to beard the old lion in his den when he defiantly stood at bay, as he often did, to give his train time, for they were invariably driven from the field by the dauntless veterans of Lexington and Drywood. Dispatches announcing the warlike situation of affairs beyond the line, were sent General McCulloch, and soon his forces were *en route* for the theater of action.

Intelligence reached us that the enemy had driven General Price beyond "Cross Hollows," and that he was making demonstrations on the town of Fayetteville. In passing the Boston mountains, the weather was intensely cold, and the men, though warmly clothed, suffered no little. On either side of the road, the precipitous mountains rose hundreds of feet overhead, while gigantic icicles hung pendant from the overhanging rocks, like huge stalactites, and, glittering in the brilliant rays of the cold winter sun, looked like the suspended spears of giants. On entering Fayetteville, the Third Regiment passed the bivouac of the Third Louisiana, our old comrades on the field of Oak Hills, who now welcomed us with extravagant demonstrations of joy. Between these two regiments there was an affectionate spirit of *comraderie*, from the battle of Oak Hills unto the last. Brigaded together during the Iuka and Corinth campaigns, the bonds of friendship became more earnest and binding with daily association. The intrepid regiment, in the veins of many of whose members the best blood of Louisiana coursed, constituted a portion of the ill-fated garrison of Vicksburg, and occupying a bastion during the siege that was blown up, its ranks were literally decimated, and but few of the intrepid and generous Frenchmen lived to return home and recount the proud story of their heroic career. The author is grateful that he has been allowed to offer even this inadequate tribute to their worth.

Great was the contrast between our entry into Fayetteville, now, and eight months before. Then, the people had faith in the puissance of the Confederate soldier, and they hailed the flag of Dixie as the harbinger of protection. Now, since defeats had destroyed the prestige of Southern arms, they looked upon our advent with apathy, seeming to think that the hand of fate was upon them, and that no earthly prowess could avert the blow. Like the French, our people grew despondent with reverses. They did not remember the high old Roman way: While the legions of Hannibal were encamped before the city, the very ground occupied by them was put up for sale to the highest bidder, as a means of obtaining funds for the prosecution of the war, and brought fabulous prices. But the despondency of the good people of Fayetteville, in the present instance, was not without foundation, for the Missouri army was in retreat, and McCulloch's infantry yet remained in position on the Van Buren road, in the Boston mountains. Halting in the town, we had the opportunity of "reviewing" the Missouri army as it defiled past us *en route* for the new position in the mountains. General Price, assuredly, had the most *multitudinous* and *variegated* wagon-train ever concentrated on the continent. Every species of wheel vehicle, from the jolting old ox-cart to the most fantastically-painted stage-coach, rolled along the road. The men were well clad, and presented a fine, soldierly appearance. Starting out, originally, as militia, the Missouri army had an entirely disproportionate number of Brigadier-Generals, and the facetious boys cried out, "Here's your army of Brigadier-Generals and stage-coaches!" The cavalry were assigned to the duty of picketing in front of the enemy, and various skirmishes, of but little interest, took place. Finally, the cavalry was withdrawn, and the enemy's cavalry occupied the town of Fayetteville for a week or two, and then fell back on Bentonville, at which place, also, was the division of Siegel. General Curtis, with the main portion of the army, occupied a very strong position, near Elk Horn tavern.

The Confederate forces, in the Boston mountains, occupied the main road leading from Van Buren to Fayetteville. The Missouri army took up position on the "Cane Hill" road. The two armies remained substantially in this position until Major-General Earl Van Dorn assumed command of both Price's and McCulloch's divisions, about March 1st, 1862. And thus a period was put to the unseemly wrangling as to precedence, that had formerly characterized the intercourse of Price and McCulloch with each other, and which, at times, very seriously impaired the efficiency of both armies. About this time, two expeditions were started to the enemy's rear, with the object of destroying whatever material of war access could be had to. Companies G and I, of the Third Regiment, commanded by Major L. S. Ross, of the Sixth Regiment, composed one of the detachments, and Company F, of the Third, was ordered to report to Major Whitfield, which, with his battalion, constituted the other. Major Ross was ordered to ride around the enemy's left wing, and Major Whitfield around the right. Ross succeeded in reaching the rear of the main force, and, at Keitsville, captured a number of prisoners, horses, and mules, and burned an immense train, containing a vast amount of military stores, and brought off his men in safety, with no loss. Major Ross won the highest compliments from the commanding General, for his dashing gallantry and skillful conduct throughout the affair. The skill and sagacity displayed in this raid, by Major Ross, gave token of that splendid career which the near future had in store for him.

Major Whitfield was not so successful, as his horses were too jaded to perform the long and rapid march necessary in affairs of this nature. On the 28th of February, General Van Dorn arrived, and assumed command of the combined Missouri and Confederate forces, and immediately preparations for an advance was then made. The army took up the line of march on the 2d of March. The weather was bitter cold, but such spirit had the new commander infused into the hearts of the men, by his energetic actions, that the signal to advance was hailed with enthusiastic shouts, and other demonstrations of joy. General Van Dorn accompanied Price's column, while General McCulloch had command of the infantry portion of his late army. General McIntosh, who had recently received his commission of Brigadier-General, commanded the cavalry. During the advance, the Sixth Regiment captured a commissary train and fifty prisoners. The march proceeded without incident, until the morning of the 5th. The weather continued cold, and snow had been falling for a day or two, and the earth was covered by the cold, white carpet, to the depth of three or four inches. Price's division had made a detour to the right, for the purpose of turning the enemy's left flank, and gaining his rear—a move that was crowned with success. McCulloch advanced upon the main road to Elk Horn tavern. McIntosh, on the left, headed for Bentonville. From the highlands, two miles south of the town, we could see Siegel's infantry retreating. Quick as thought, we obliqued to the left, and passed around the town, having for an object the cutting off of Siegel's division. But the cunning old fox, calculating exactly where we would enter the road again, placed his division, 10,000 strong, in ambush, and the first intimation we had of the position of affairs, was the firing upon our advance-guard, Company B, Third Regiment, Captain Cumby commanding. The Third Regiment was in the advance, and the men apprehensive of no danger. Many were walking, leading their horses, to get warm by the exercise. Bang! bang! went the guns, fired at Cumby's company, and, quick as thought, McIntosh drew his saber and ordered the bugle to sound the charge. It may be imagined that the regiment was thrown into great disorder. Yet, the impetuous young general led the assault, sword in hand, up to the very muzzles of Siegel's guns. A deafening roar of artillery, and rattling of musketry, greeted the charging column, and minnie-balls, grape and canister chorused through the air. *The regiment was repulsed!* Had such a thing been whispered before as possible, every man in the regiment would have denounced him as a calumniator, who mouthed the suspicion. The intrepid McIntosh, amid a shower of balls, grasped the flag, and, waving it above his head, implored the men to rally for another charge. But brave, simple-hearted old Captain Hale stood up in his stirrups, the tears trickling down his snow-white beard, and exclaimed: "*This here rigiment are disgraced forever! . I'd a ruther died right thar than to a give arry a inch!*" Brave old Captain Hale! He was a diamond in the rough, and his men regarded him more in the light of a kind father than that of an officer, and when the time came for the election of officers, after the first year's service had expired, his "boys" begged him to remain with them as their Captain. We were serving, then, as infantry, and the feeble old hero informed them that he could not make one day's march afoot. Whereupon, the "boys" held a consultation, and it was determined upon that they would purchase their beloved old Captain a horse and buggy! Did ever man govern before with such unanimous and full consent of the governed? The loss of the regiment in this affair was ten men killed and twenty wounded. The command camped at "Camp Stephens" the night of the 5th. The snow fell all night. The command was in motion two hours before day, and all felt assured that a few hours would usher in the first act of the drama. *En route* to the field of battle, we passed the Indian Brigade of General Pike, all of whom were painted, in conformity to the horrid custom of their people. Soon the thunders of Price's guns announced that the "Old Guard" were in position, in the enemy's rear, and General McCulloch at once advanced a brigade of infantry, composed of the Third Louisiana and several regiments of Arkansas troops, against the Federal left. As McIntosh, at the head of several cavalry regiments, came on the field, marching by fours, in the following order: Third Texas on the right; Sixth Texas on the right center; Ninth Texas on the left center; and Brooks' battalion on the left, through an open field, in parallel lines, by fours, a Federal battery, supported by a brigade of infantry, opened upon us at a distance of about 500 yards. General Ben. McCulloch was just passing the Third Regiment, with a Confederate battery, and, as the first Yankee shell went crashing through our ranks, commanded, "Wheel that battery into line!"—probably the last order ever uttered by this true and staunch son of Texas. The gallant McIntosh ordered the bugle to sound the charge, and, waving his saber overhead, led the furious and irresistible charge. Like the impetuous rush of an avalanche, the mad columns swept over the field, in the midst of a tempest of iron hail, the thunders of artillery, the yells of the combatants, and the groans of the dying and wounded. They are upon the enemy! and the iron dogs of war are hushed. The combatants become intermixed, and the gunners are cut down at their posts. The Stars and Stripes go down, and the Red Cross of the South waves in triumph above the scene of destruction. But the work of slaughter does not stop here. The infuriated cavaliers charge the supporting infantry, in the teeth of a most destructive storm of musketry, and, routed, they fly from the field! The Third Regiment did not engage in the brilliant affair, as it remained to support the Confederate battery before alluded to. By this time, McCulloch's infantry were warmly engaged with the enemy, about eight hundred yards in front of Pea Ridge, and the interminable volleys of musketry told how hotly contested was the fight. The Third Regiment was dismounted, and placed in line of battle just behind the crest of Pea Ridge, as a support to the infantry, and with orders not to abandon the Ridge under any circumstances. General McCulloch, very early in the action, imprudently ventured too far in front of his own lines, to reconnoiter the enemy's position, and this was the last ever seen of the brave and conscientious old Texas chief in life. The impetuous McIntosh, who was at home only amidst the raging of wild elements, and who courted the missions of danger with a fondness not surpassed by the affection of a lover for his mistress, led an Arkansas regiment of infantry against the enemy, soon after his dashing cavalry charge, and fell at the very muzzles of their guns, sword in hand. The author regrets exceedingly that he has no *data* upon which to predicate any sketch of the life of this daring young Georgian. He was the soul of honor and chivalry; the *beau sabreur* of the Western army; and, had he lived, would have written his name high upon the memorial roll of Fame. With McIntosh, there was no intermediate rest between death and glory. To add to the misfortunes of the Confederate forces, on this ill-starred field, Colonel Hebert, of the Third Louisiana, who, after McIntosh, was the next ranking officer in McCulloch's division, was taken prisoner. It was evident, from the firing, that the brave old

Missourian was slowly driving the main force of the enemy before his indomitable "Grizzly Bears," and the unbroken succession of the volleys from cannon and rifles, which sounded like one continuous roll of thunder, proclaimed the deadly nature of the conflict. And had McCulloch and McIntosh lived; had Hebert been spared us; or had Colonel Greer known that the carnival of death and misfortune had devolved the command upon himself; the enemy before us, too, would have been driven back upon a common center, where but the alternative of surrender or destruction awaited the Federal army. As it was, these brave Louisianians and Arkansians, without a head, manfully breasted the terrific storm of shot and canister poured into their ranks by an enemy who outnumbered them in the ratio of five to one, throughout the entire day, and yielded never one foot of ground. The continued absence of Generals McCulloch and McIntosh excited the suspicions of Colonel Greer that all was not right, and he dispatched private John N. Coleman, of Company A, Third Regiment, to go in quest of the Generals, and ascertain if no further disposition of the reserve was to be made, for that experienced officer well knew that the brave and weary Louisianians and Arkansians in our front should be re-enforced, or relieved by a fresh division entirely.

Mr. Coleman soon returned, saying that he could ascertain nothing in regard to the whereabouts of either Generals McCulloch or McIntosh, but that he had seen the Adjutant-General of each, neither of whom could give any account of their chieftains. Mr. Coleman, however, stated that he had met Lieutenant-Colonel Lane, who had been detached from his regiment, and placed in command of another cavalry corps; that Lane wished Greer to meet him at a log-house, immediately in rear of his brigade, where they could hold a consultation, and arrive at some determination as to what course should be pursued in the strange and anomalous state of affairs. Thither Colonel Greer repaired, without the loss of any precious time. It was decided by these officers, to withdraw the troops to the main road, about one-half mile in rear of our present position, and dispatch a courier to General Van Dorn, announcing the critical condition in which this wing of the army was placed. At 11 P. M., with no guard but the friendly darkness, Mr. John N. Coleman set out on his hazardous mission, in the prosecution of which it was necessary to describe the semi-circumference of the circle of which the enemy's center was the pivot, and pass his flank, all the while exposed to imminent danger of being captured by the cavalry covering that wing of the army. Coleman arrived at General Van Dorn's head-quarters at one o'clock, with the dispatches, which imparted the first intelligence to the General that all was not right with McCulloch's division. General Van Dorn instructed his Assistant Adjutant-General, Major Dabney H. Maury, to write Colonel Greer an order, directing him to withdraw the entire division, and lead it around the enemy's right flank, to the position occupied by the Missouri division. Coleman, with a sagacity superior to that of his chief, refused to bear the order in writing, for, if he was captured, and unable to destroy the paper, the enemy would come into possession of the fact that some calamity had occurred to that division, and at once inaugurate measures to prevent the desired concentration, when General Van Dorn consented that it should be transmitted verbally. Coleman returned about 2 A. M., and Colonel Greer at once undertook the hazardous task of complying with the directions of General Van Dorn. Mr. Coleman, for the eminent services rendered on this occasion, was recommended by Colonel Greer for promotion, and was, accordingly, commissioned Regimental Commissary of Subsistence, with the rank of Captain. Subsequently, on the formation of the Texas Brigade, he was named Commissary for the Brigade, with the rank of Major. He deserved the highest meed of praise for the cool courage, devotion to the cause, and penetrating sagacity manifested on this occasion. Major Coleman had the misfortune to lose both his feet, a few years ago, by a railway accident. He resides in the city of Marshall, Harrison county, Texas, respected by all his neighbors, and beloved by his comrades of the old Brigade. The division reached the head-quarters of General Van Dorn about daylight, and, after a few sporadic charges on the enemy, and some desultory firing, apparently without spirit or object, the "Army of the West," which had never before turned its back to the foe, sullenly retired from the scene, leaving the defeated enemy in possession of the field. Van Dorn was urgently pressed by General Beauregard, the Department Commander, to re-enforce him at Corinth, Mississippi, with all his available force, for almost simultaneously with the battle of Elk Horn, the terrible tragedy of Shiloh had been enacted, and General Beauregard was now confronted by an overwhelming force, commanded by Major-General Halleck. Van Dorn acted with haste, but so consummate had been all his preparations, that, had it not been for the death of McCulloch and McIntosh, the battle of Elk Horn would have been one of the most crushing defeats to the enemy known in modern times; for, surrounded as he was, defeat meant capitulation or destruction. Even had he organized a continued and vigorous attack by the combined divisions, the evening of March 8th, 1862, would have ushered into history a splendid Confederate victory. The soldiers, every one of whom felt that the beaten enemy was not entitled to the possession of the field of battle, and its necessary sequence—the meed of victory—quitted the contest with reluctance, feeling that they had been defrauded of their well-earned dues, and many were the anxious glances turned to the rear by the retreating army, in the vain hope that the enemy would attempt a pursuit. But nothing was more distant from the intentions of General Curtis and his Lieutenants. They had had sufficient work, and were content to let "good enough alone." "By the gods!" exclaimed "Colonel" H. McBride Pridgen, a private of Whitfield's battalion, in describing the battle to friends at home, "we whipped them! we butchered them! we extirminated them! and I don't believe there was but one man that escaped to tell the tale, and *he* stole my blankets!" Upon this statement of the gallant "Colonel" Pridgen, "hangs a tale."

Whitfield's battalion had been dismounted, in order that it could participate in the battle as infantry, which it did, and, as the Third Regiment was marching to the battle-field, on the morning of the 6th, "Colonel" Pridgen, who, foot-sore and weary, had sat down by the roadside, enveloped in a huge, gray, double blanket, in one corner of which was worked, in scarlet worsted, "H. McBride Pridgen." Being acquainted with nearly every man in Company A, he desired some one to allow him to ride behind him to the battle-field. Robert R. Wright invited the fatigued man to mount behind him, which he did, and rejoined his command on the battle-field. In the heat of the action, his huge blankets became too cumbersome, and he laid them on the ground, but the line being forced back by the enemy, the "Colonel's" blankets were not recovered. He gave them up for lost, and, at the dreary bivouac fire, often afterwards spoke in touching terms of his friendly blankets. Time wore on, and Van Dorn's command was transferred to Mississippi, and had the honor of whipping the *corps d'armee* of "Head-Quarters-in-the-Saddle" Pope, at the battle of Farmington, capturing his camp and all its contents. After the battle, the boys engaged, to a moderate extent, in pillaging his deserted stores. Imagine my surprise, when the redoubtable "Colonel" Pridgen rushed up, holding a large, double, gray blanket in his hands, in the corner of which still shone the legend in crimson letters: "H. McBride Pridgen!" "By the gods!" he exclaimed, "I have found the blankets I lost at Elk Horn, Arkansas." This was a strange coincidence, but the circumstance is true.

The bodies of the slain generals were recovered from the field by members of their respective staffs. It is believed that the body of the lamented young Georgian was buried in Van Buren, Arkansas, and that of General McCulloch, conveyed to Texas, by Colonel Brown, his old friend, and a member of his staff. General Ben. McCulloch came to Texas, at a very early day, and fought at the battle of San Jacinto. He was a celebrated Indian fighter, and, among other creditable affairs with the savage foe, defeated the daring band of Comanches that burned Linnville, in the battle of Plum Creek, in the year 1840. Subsequently, he engaged in the Mexican war, as commandant of a guerrilla battalion, that performed many eminent services during the war. As a citizen, Ben. McCulloch had the respect and confidence of all who knew him. He filled several public positions of trust, and acquitted himself, in the discharge of his duties, with as much credit to the probity of his character as to his business capacity. He was among the first appointments of Mr. Davis, receiving the commission of Brigadier-General, and was assigned to the command of the Arkansas District—a command involving, probably, more vexatious questions for solution than any other in the Confederate States. To say that General McCulloch acquitted himself with credit in his administration of the affairs of his district, and that he retained the confidence of his government to the last, is eulogium sufficient to satisfy his most exacting friend. General McCulloch was very abstemious in his appetites, and indulged in none of the small vices. The character of none of the sons of Texas could more properly be chosen as an exemplar for the youth of the land. Ben. McCulloch was dear to all true Texans. May the grass grow green above his soldier-mound!

# CHAPTER V.

RETREAT FROM ELK HORN—RESCUE OF ARTILLERY—EMBARKATION AT DUVALL'S BLUFF—MEMPHIS—CORINTH, ETC., ETC.

The soldierly conduct of Private Polk Dye, of Company F, Third Texas Cavalry, in the battle of Elk Horn, deserves mention. Having lost his horse, he joined temporarily a company of the Third Louisiana Infantry, and stood the brunt of battle with that noble regiment all day. In the last of many charges made by the regiment, his arm was broken by a minnie-bullet. He was assisted to his own regiment by his comrades of the day, who paid him high compliments for his coolness and courage.

As our wagon-train had been ordered back to the Arkansas river, when Colonel Greer made the move to rejoin General Van Dorn, the command was without rations, and the men presented the most gloomy and dejected appearance possible to conceive. By some unaccountable oversight, the entire park of artillery belonging to McCulloch's late division, in withdrawing from the field, were suffered to take a road leading to the north. Just as we had bivouaced, after the third day's march, hungry, gloomy, and dispirited, orders came for the Third Regiment to saddle up and return in quest of the artillery, which had been heard from, and to escort it to the army. Mechanically the men obeyed, and were soon retracing their march in gloomy silence. In the morning we met Captain Good, having in charge his own and other batteries. Instead of losing our own artillery, as many feared was the case, we ascertained that we had brought off one more piece than we had carried on the field. Finally, after many days' wrestling with the "grim and unrelenting enemy," hunger, we reached our winter-quarters, where the wagon-train awaited us, with an abundance of rations. Replenishing the inner man, we hurriedly resumed the march for Little Rock, and from thence to Duvall's Bluff, at which place, to our utter astonishment, we were ordered to be dismounted, our horses sent to Texas, and the men embarked on a steamboat and transported to Memphis, Tenn., *en route* to Corinth, Miss. Notwithstanding the fact that we regarded this order as a breach of faith, totally at variance with our contract, yet the men being impressed with a correct idea of the critical condition in which recent reverses had placed the Confederacy, yielded their own inclinations, with patriotic zeal and devotion to the cause, and complied. The Third Regiment embarked on board the steamboat "Scotland," and soon were steaming down White river. The stream was flooded to overflowing, as was the "old father of waters." After a trip without incident, the regiment arrived at Memphis, and encamped in the suburbs of the city for several days. Finally, we departed by train for Corinth, and soon reached that disease-infected point. Here General Beauregard was in command of an army variously estimated at from 35,000 to 75,000 men. We opine the former figures came nearest the truth.

Without memoranda or *data* of any nature of the other regiments that subsequently composed the brigade, a narrative of whose services we are purposing now to commit to paper, can not be followed through all their individual movements, as can that one of which the author was a member; and if, seemingly, more prominence is given the Third than to the others, the author would beg his comrades to assign the effect to the cause just stated. He would not detract one iota from the well-earned fame of any. To him the Legion—Ninth, Sixth, and Third—are one, and he only wishes he could be invested with the means of according even-handed justice to all, as assuredly he has the will to do so. At Corinth, the Third Regiment was placed in a newly-organized brigade, over which was placed Brigadier-General Hogg. General Hogg was a Texas gentleman of many commendable social and domestic qualities, and was a veteran of the Mexican war, having served as a private in Wood's regiment. General Hogg soon fell a victim to the brooding malaria of that plague-infected place.

Colonel Louis Hebert, of the Third Louisiana, though a prisoner in the hands of the enemy, was promoted Brigadier-General, and to this brigade the Third Texas Regiment was transferred. The brigade, in the absence of General Hebert, was commanded by Colonel J. W. Whitfield, of the First Texas Legion. This brigade did not participate in any of the actual fighting at the battle of Farmington, in which the vain-glorious Pope was driven back, in disgrace, by one division of Van Dorn's *corps d'armee*, and his camp captured, though it did an unpleasant amount of marching, with the object of cutting Pope off from the ford of Hatchie creek. But that doughty warrior was too fast for us, as we arrived just in time to witness the crossing of his rear-guard. Thus, time passed in drilling, skirmishing, and *physicing*, —for fully one-half of the men were prostrated by camp dysentery— until May 8, 1862, which day had been designated as the time for the re-organization of the regiment, by the election of field and company officers: Captain Robert H. Cumby, of Company B, was elected Colonel; Captain H. P. Mabry, of Company G, Lieutenant-Colonel; and Captain Barker, Major. Dr. Zeb. Shaw was appointed Surgeon; J. N. Coleman, Captain and Commissary; E. P. Hill, Quartermaster; O. N. Hollingsworth, Adjutant, and Wm. H. Gee, Sergeant-Major.

A. B. Stone, Captain Co. A; Giles S. Boggess, Captain Co. B; James Jones, Captain Co. C; R. S. Dabney, Captain Co. D; Preston B. Ward, Captain Co. E; R. F. Dunn, Captain Co. F; S. C. Noble, Captain Co. G; J. W. Lee, Captain Co. H; —— Green, Captain Co. I; Sid. S. Johnston, Captain Co. K.

As both Colonel Cumby and Lieutenant-Colonel Mabry were in bad health, and unable to assume the command, Major Barker requested Colonel Lane to retain command of the regiment awhile longer, to which request Colonel Lane consented.

During this campaign, the enemy advanced his lines slowly and with the greatest caution; for he had been made to feel the steel of his less numerous opponent on the sanguinary field of Shiloh, and to respect his prowess. Disease was the insidious and fatal enemy that the Southern army had to yield to, finally. Day by day, the ranks of the men on duty grew thinner and thinner. The hospitals were crowded, and thousands were sent to asylums far in the rear. The evacuation was voluntary, on the part of General Beauregard, and dictated by the soundest policy. The movement was affected in the face of the enemy, without confusion or the loss of a cartridge. Preparatory to this retrograde move, the trains were so taxed, in the removal of supplies and munitions of war, that many of the sick could not obtain transportation, and these poor unfortunates were the 10,000 prisoners alleged to have been captured by Major-General "Head-quarters-in-the-Saddle" Pope, over which he crowed so lustily in the papers of the North, and for which he was considered the hero to instruct the Army of the Potomac in the ways to victory—with what success, the reader knows who has perused an account of his passage at arms with brave old "Stonewall" Jackson, at second Manassas.

Previous to the retreat, there transpired many acts of daring and intrepidity on the part of Southern commands in the innumerable skirmishes, and affairs of outposts, that daily occurred. In one of several, the cool courage and soldierly bearing of the Third was so marked as to call from the commanding General a complimentary notice that was read on parade to the entire army. On June 29th, heavy skirmishing was going on in our immediate front, and the regiment was ordered out to support the skirmishers. On the advanced skirmish line the command was drawn up in line of battle, and an advance ordered by Lieutenant-Colonel Lane, who, on the right, led the men in person, while the brave and young Major Barker, performed a similar duty on the left. The firing increased in volume as the regiment advanced, until Colonel Lane ordered the charge, which was responded to by deafening yells on the part of the men. A deadly volley of musketry was poured into the line of yelling, charging Texans, who, with bayonets fixed, rushed, with the impetuosity of a tornado, over all obstructions, and, though numbering but 256 rifles, drove the Eleventh Ohio and Eighteenth Missouri infantry regiments, numbering full 1,000 men, in confusion and dismay, from the field. The regiment sustained a loss of thirty killed and fifty-five wounded. Among the former was the brave young Major Barker, whose high soldierly bearing on this and former occasions, won the admiration of all. The contest was warm, short, and decisive, as thirty minutes would have covered the whole time of the entire action.

The author can not refrain from reproducing, in this connection, a vivid discription of this gallant action, from the pen of Judge Hogg, who was a member of the Third Texas Regiment:

"On the morning preceding the evacuation of Corinth by the Confederates under Beauregard, in May, 1862, we made a considerable demonstration on the front of our lines, in order to hoodwink the enemy, while the *materiel* and main bulk of the troops were withdrawn. Among the forces ordered out was the Third Texas Cavalry, dismounted, under command of Colonel W. P. Lane. About sunrise on the 28th of May, the regiment was ordered to "double-quick" to re-enforce the skirmishers, who were being heavily pressed by a force of the enemy of vast numerical superiority. After passing through an immense *abatis* and over a formidable *chevaux de frise*, we came up with our advanced skirmishers, and in full view of the enemy's position, which was in a valley about three hundred yards distant, covered by a jungle of black-jack underbrush that completely veiled them from our view, while our position afforded no cover except large oaks, and we were denied their protection when it interfered with our alignment. As soon as we were discovered by the enemy, a galling fire was opened upon our line, and from the volumes of smoke that boiled up from the copse, and the deafening roar of the musketry, we were apprised of the fact that the encounter would be stubborn and deadly. The battle opened in earnest, now, and the firing became terrific. There were only 246 of our regiment well enough to participate in the engagement, and, owing to the ememy's heavy overbalance of numbers, and their more advantageous position, it behooved every man to avail himself of whatever protection the timber afforded. Each man took his tree, and, after discharging his fire-lock and re-loading in that position, would advance to the next cover and repeat the performance. Colonel W. P. Lane, Major James A. J. Barker, and Adjutant Orlando Hollingsworth were the only mounted officers on the field, and, thus exposed, were excellent targets for the enemy's sharpshooters. We advanced but a short distance in the aforesaid manner, when Lane's favorite command, "Charge!" was given, to dislodge the enemy from his stronghold. At the spell-word, "charge," each Texan quit his cover, and dashed with wonted impetuosity upon the opposing ranks. The forest resounded with their dreadful shout, which sent a chill of terror to the hearts of the invaders. In full run, the Texans, with the fury of madmen, close on the lurking enemy, whose skill and power are spent in vain to check them. Over three thousand rifles are belching forth their death-fraught charges into the slim line of the brave 246—still they come! Their wake is covered with the best blood of the nation—yet on they rush! They reach the fire-breathing thicket, and, without a halt, they plunge into its thorny bosom, when, in one chaotic stampede, the gallant brigade of Indianians, that Uncle Sam had entrusted with honor's post, made their shameful exeunt, leaving about forty of their dead and a like number of their wounded on the field. The flying enemy was pursued until the sound of the "long roll" in the main camp, warned the impetuous Lane that prudence counseled a halt. Of the boys from Cherokee, we found the brave young Abner Harris dead; Wallace Caldwell—the beloved, the noble Wallace—languishing under a mortal wound, and John Lambert severely wounded.

"Many were lamented on that day, but none more than that prince of nature's nobleman, the talented and chivalric Major James A. J. Barker, the pride of his regiment. He fell while gallantly cheering his men on to victory, as he had done on many a well-fought field. His gallantry and general superiority was the theme of every tongue that knew him. His name was inseparably connected with our ideas of valor, magnanimity, truth, candor, and fidelity.

"The Major had a presentiment of evil, and so informed his intimate friends on the morning of the battle. The dying hero fell into the arms of John Myres and Lem. Reed, who bore his inanimate form from the field of his death and his glory."

The author made many attempts to obtain a copy of the complimentary address issued to the army, by General Beauregard, on this occasion, but regrets that all his efforts were unavailing. If such a copy is extant, he hopes to be able to procure it, should a second edition of this work be demanded.

## CHAPTER VI.

General Beauregard executed the movement of retiring from Corinth in a masterly manner. Captain S. S. Johnston, Company K, of the Third, was on picket duty at the time of withdrawal, and, in the hurry of the moment, Colonel Lane neglected to relieve them. The army had proceeded some miles when the absence of gallant old Company K was remarked. The courier who bore Captain Johnston the order to "fall back," found him, with his twenty-five Texans, boldly confronting Halleck's 100,000. Texas had many brave and daring sons to be proud of, but not one more deservedly so than Captain Sid. S. Johnston—now the modest, unassuming citizen of Tyler, Texas.

General Halleck seemed satisfied with the occupation of Corinth, and halted his victorious legions at that point.

The Confederate army retired to Tupelo, on the Mobile and Ohio railroad. The greater portion was soon transferred, under General Bragg, to Tennessee. One *corps de armee* remained at Tupelo, composed of the divisions of Generals Maury and Little, the whole commanded by Major-General Sterling Price. For several months, the corps remained here, with no incident to break the dull monotony save the daily "guard mounting" and drill. About the time General Bragg commenced his advance into Kentucky, the camp was removed up the railroad to Saltillo, about fifteen miles north of Tupelo. From this point General Price made a rapid march on Iuka, where General Rosecranz was posted with about 10,000 men—General Grant being at Corinth, fifteen miles above, with as many more. So complete was the surprise, that General Rosecranz evacuated the town without removing or destroying any of his immense stores collected there. Consequently, the Confederates reveled on "Yankee" rations during their short-lived possession of the place. Price's position was an extremely hazardous one here, and not a night passed but an alarm was sounded. Our cavalry was extremely inefficient, and the enemy was expected on either of three fronts. When the crisis came, after a week of anxious watch, the army was drawn up in line of battle on the Corinth road, about three miles from Iuka, awaiting the enemy, who, it was reported, was advancing on that road. When, suddenly, a breathless courier dashed up to General Price with the astounding information that the enemy was advancing on Iuka from the south side, and that nothing interposed between him and the town save a company of cavalry, who could offer him no opposition. Hebert's Brigade, composed of the First Texas Legion, Third Texas Cavalry (dismounted), Third Louisiana Infantry, and Fortieth Mississippi Infantry—the whole commanded by General Louis Hebert—was ordered to "double-quick" to the threatened point. Arriving, the Third Texas was deployed as skirmishers, and drove the Federal sharpshooters back on the reserve. The brigade was now formed in line of battle, and King's (Confederate) battery opened fire. This was immediately responded to by the enemy's artillery; at the same time, the firing of small arms became general, and, as the opposing lines were not exceeding three hundred yards apart, considerable execution was done. As Generals Price and Little were conferring, just in the rear of the Third Texas, the latter received a rifle-ball in the forehead and fell from his horse into the arms of Sergeant T. J. Cellum, of Company A, Third Texas, dead. General Price dismounted and hastened to the side of the fallen general, whose spirit, alas, had already flown. To Cellum, the old hero said, with moistened eyes and husky voice: "Bear his body from the field, my son; and remain with it, yourself, until I can join you." That night, when the storm of battle had lulled, the form of General Little was consigned to a hastily-dug grave, "by the light of the lanterns dimly burning."

A forward movement was now ordered, and as the brigade marched with slow and solemn tread down a slight declivity in the direction of the enemy, a little dog was observed trotting along in advance of the line, apparently oblivious to the thunders of artillery, the rattle of rifles, and the whizzing of missiles that literally filled the air. The fate of the brave little rebel dog was never known. Arriving at the base of the declivity, the command "double-quick," was given. The enemy now redoubled his exertions. Nine pieces of artillery were brought to bear, and the threatened point re-enforced. "Charge!" was the next command uttered by brave little creole Hebert, and the Confederates, yelling like demons reveling in a saturnalia of death, pushed forward at the top of their speed. They are met, full in the face, by the iron contents of the nine cannon, and, like a tree torn by the hurricane, waver for a moment. "On, men, on!" shouts the impetuous Frenchman, and the Confederates distinctly hear the command of the enemy: "Double charge of grape and canister!" They know what the result will be if the cannon are not taken before they can be again fired. Their comrades lie around them dead and dying. Of five colonels, not one remains. Death is abroad in his fury; *but to retreat is more dangerous than to advance!* The men hesitate but a moment, and raising again the demoniac yell, dash madly forward and reach the guns just as the double load is being driven home. In vain did the infantry support attempt to come to the rescue of the guns—their charges on the Confederate line were as impotent as the beating of the waves on the sides of Gibraltar. The Confederate loss was simply terrible. In the Legion and Third Texas, one-third of the men were killed or wounded. Their loss was greater from the fact that their position was immediately in front of the death-dealing artillery.

Where all displayed such heroism, it would seem invidious to make distinctions;' but the author can not refrain from mentioning the name of brave young Lieutenant Dan. H. Alley, of Company G, Third Texas, who he witnessed, in the hottest period of the charge, sword in hand, calling to his men, "Come on, boys!"

Colonel H. P. Mabry, commanding Third Texas, received a severe wound that fractured an ankle; Colonel J. W. Whitfield was wounded severely in the shoulder; Colonel Gillam, of the Third Louisiana, received a half-dozen wounds, that incapacitated him for active service. Captain Odell, Brigade Commissary, was killed.

The author feels excusable in mentioning the death of his friend, John Sherrod, who was killed at his side—a grape-shot passing entirely through the body.

Night put an end to the carnage. General Price became convinced that General Grant had re-enforced General Rosecranz, and that his retreat would be cut off, resolved to anticipate events, and about 9 P. M., commenced a retrograde movement in the direction of Baldwin, Mississippi. The enemy did not attempt a pursuit, as he was satisfied with the test of metal at Iuka. All the wounded, unable to march, fell into the hands of the enemy. But, at this period, the humane system of paroling prisoners was in operation, and it was not until some months later that both sides disgraced the American name, and libelled humanity, in their inhuman treatment of prisoners.

A characteristic anecdote is told of Colonel Mabry, who fell into the enemy's hands. The printed parole offered him to sign, read "the so-called Confederate States," etc. The punctilious officer refused to attach his name to the instrument, alleging that the Confederacy was an established fact; and as Colonel Mabry was about as firm in his convictions as old Cato of Rome, he was given a parole in which the obnoxious words did not occur. And all Confederate soldiers will remember that their paroles, at the general surrender, read "Confederate States," etc.—a phraseology of respect accorded to the punctilious honor and manly firmness of Colonel H. P. Mabry, of Texas.

An incident in regard to General Hebert: As the Third Texas was being thrown forward as skirmishers—the enemy still advancing and firing—an officer of the regiment asked of the General, who was superintending the movement, "General, must we fix bayonets?" "Yes, sir!" shouted the impatient officer; "What for you have ze bayonet, if you no fix him? Yes, by gar; fix him! fix him!"

At Baldwin, General Price was met by General Earl Van Dorn, who had advanced from Vicksburg with about 5,000 men—General Price's force was about twice as many. With this force, General Van Dorn, who now assumed the command, commenced a rapid advance on Corinth—probably the strongest fortified place in the South—occupied by General Rosecranz and 30,000 men. The fatiguing march was attended by no incident until the morning of the first day's fight, when, just at daybreak, three distinct shocks of an earthquake were felt, and construed by many as of ominous import.

It is not the province of the author, in this connection, to give the details of operation unconnected with the immediate operations of the four regiments that composed Ross' Brigade; and as that brigade had not yet been organized, difficulty is experienced in correctly drawing the line. Suffice it to say, the four regiments participated in this fatal battle, and bore themselves, as they always did, with soldierly daring and bravery. They charged the outer line of breastworks, over *abatis* of fallen timber; they scaled the works through bristling rows of *chevaux de frise*, and silenced the seige guns on the ramparts by capture. During the night of the first day's fight, the Confederate army was drawn up in line of battle, Price occupying the center, and bivouaced on their arms. The signal for attack the next morning was a discharge of ten pieces of artillery by Price. As agreed upon, the ten cannon were discharged simultaneously, just at daybreak, and the army rose to its feet as one man. A desperate charge was immediately made upon the inner lines, which were also taken in many places, though at a fearful cost of life. All know how short-lived was this ephemeral success. It is enough to recount the catastrophe, without attempting to designate the cause. The charging columns were not supported as they should have been, and were, consequently, driven from the town, to which they had penetrated in the frenzy of the charge, and back across the breastworks, which they had purchased at such a fearful cost, only to lose again. That some one was culpable, is not to be disputed; but to designate the individual is the province of the general historian, and not the author of this circumscribed narrative.

A disorderly retreat was now commenced, with the enemy in close pursuit. Villepigue's Brigade, only, of the whole army, preserved sufficient discipline to interpose any impediment in the way of the triumphant enemy.

In advancing on Corinth, General Van Dorn had left the wagon-trains at the bridge on the Hatchie river; and the Texas Legion, consisting of about 500 efficient men, together with other detachments, numbering possibly 500 more, constituted the guard left to preserve the sole means of retreat, and secure the train from capture. And now, to add to the gravity of the situation, Generals Hulburt and Ord came down from Grand Junction with a corps about 10,000 fresh men, rendered enthusiastic by the news of the victory, and gained possession of the bridge, after an obstinate contest with the guard; in which action the "Old Legion" bore itself with conspicuous gallantry, and suffered heavily in killed, wounded, and prisoners.

Previous to the capture of the bridge, however, Colonel L. S. Ross, in command of a brigade numbering not more than 700 rifles for duty, were thrown across the stream to support the Confederate guard, commanded by Brigadier-General Moore, who was overwhelmed by numbers, and his heterogeneous force almost disorganized, ere the arrival of Ross. Moore urged Ross to retire behind the stream, and pointed out the futility of his sustaining an attack from the advancing enemy, who numbered near 10,000 fresh men. Colonel Ross maintained his position, however, until his superior in rank, General Maury, ordered a retreat. To extricate his brigade from the hazardous position it now occupied, demanded prudence, skill, and courage, and that Colonel Ross effected this delicate maneuver, in the face of overwhelming numbers of troops flushed with victory, speaks volumes in his praise.

The triumphant enemy now held the bridge, and nothing intervened between him and the Confederate wagon-train but Ross and his little brigade, who maintained their position with a heroism not excelled by either side during the whole course of the war. Finally, General Maury brought up the brigades of Generals Phifer and Cabell, and this force kept the enemy at bay, during a brief crisis in the history of the Army of the West, that momentarily threatened a disastrous catastrophe. The routed and disorganized columns of Van Dorn and Price, closely pursued by Rosecranz, were now arriving upon the scene in a state of demoralization that made "confusion worse confounded." In the rear of this straggling mass, the gallant Villepigue, at the head of his brigade, was offering such opposition to Rosecranz as his paucity of numbers would justify. But neither Villepigue nor Maury could hope to maintain their positions, against such fearful odds, long.

It appeared that the "Army of the West" was confronting its fate at last on the banks of this turbid and impassable stream. Events had reached a crisis, and disaster seemed imminent. Generals Van Dorn and Price hold a hurried interview. The head of the column is turned to the left of the road, and the forlorn retreat is resumed down the river. A mounted detachment is hastened down the stream to a point some ten miles distant, where the remains of an ancient mill-dam are said to exist. Upon this foundation, the "pioneers" hastily improvise a bridge ere the head of the column appears. Over this providential bridge the army passes, and frees itself from the enveloping folds of the enemy. A sigh of relief escapes ten thousand hearts when they realize their escape from the very jaws of destruction. Strange to relate, not a wagon was lost, not a gun—though so demoralized was the army that, had the enemy maintained a vigorous pursuit, the consequences must have proved fatal to the Confederates. General Rosecranz, with the humanity characteristic of the brave, caused the Confederate dead, upon the fields of Corinth and Hatchie, to be properly interred. The brave Colonel Rodgers, of the Second Texas Infantry, who fell, sword in hand, upon the death-swept ramparts, the foremost man in one of the deadliest assaults of modern times, was accorded a soldier's burial, with all the honors of war, by his admiring enemies. Such acts as this, half redeems the depravity of man, and partially beguiles the horrors of war. The beaten army retired to Holly Springs; where, however, it was not suffered long to remain, as General Grant, who has been rather appropriately styled the "Modern Sphynx," placed his legions in motion, with the city of Vicksburg as the objective point.

It was evident to the most obtuse, that the fortunes of the Confederacy in that quarter were desperate, and that, unless something extraordinary was attempted, Vicksburg must become the prey of the Federals. The defeated army contained, in its own ranks, the medium through which its deliverance was to be obtained. Three thousand five hundred cavalrymen were destined to achieve this result—an exploit unsurpassed in the annals of war, and which revolutionized the art of war in America, at least, by assigning the cavalry-arm to a position of importance it had never before occupied.

For his defeat at Corinth, Major-General Earl Van Dorn was superseded in the command of the "Army of the West" by Lieutenant-General J. C. Pemberton.

### ROSS' BRIGADE.

#### I.

No more the bugle's ringing blast,
  Now sounds "to horse!" throughout the camp;
No more the charger, dashing fast,
  In gore his quiv'ring fetlocks tramp;
No more the "Red Cross" proudly waves
  Defiance to the haughty foe;
No more the crimson battle waves
  Of human blood, now ebb and flow.

#### II.

No more as when the "cool Old Chief,"*
  His life gave up in sacrifice,
Does glory lead the path to grief,
  Where tears and sobs may not suffice;
No more as when the "dashing boy,"†
  A stranger, came to do and dare,
Is life exchanged for fame's alloy,
  Like empty bubbles, light as air.

---

* "Cool Old Chief"—General Ben. McCulloch.
† "The Dashing Boy"—General McIntosh, killed at Elk Horn.

### III.

Still we recall those scenes with pride,
  And mark each incident, though light;
The bivouac, the cheerless ride,
  The skirmish, and the deadly fight.
*First in the front of each advance,*
  *Last in the rear of each retreat;*
The Cossack Ranger's ready lance,
  Was ever poised the foe to meet.

### IV.

And when the "modern Sphynx" arrayed—
  With will to match against the fates—
His legions which had ne'er essayed
  In vain the storm of city gates,
Delay'd, proud Vicksburg, was thy doom,
  By spectral men on noiseless wings,
Who lit, with lurid glare, the gloom,
  That hung a pall o'er Holly Springs.

### V.

A pandemonium, Spring Hill heard,
  When Whitfield led, through shot and shell,
The "Legion," "Sixth," the "Ninth," and "Third,"
  And triumphed o'er a mimic hell.
With Yazoo glories, bursts enlarge,
  As recompense for all our loss,
Where fortune, in the dashing charge,
  Conferr'd the "wreath and stars"* on Ross.

### VI.

Around the lines of Corinth, where
  Disease, an ally of the foe,
Rode on the pestilential air,
  And claimed its dues of death and woe;
And 'round Atlanta's ditches red,
  Where Valor failed to cope with Might,
We left at rest our priceless dead,
  Athwart the field from left to right.

---

° "Wreath and stars"—insignia of a general officer.

## VII.

No marble shaft may point the way,
 No epitaph the tombs disclose,
Where death's still line, in grim array,
 Unheeded find their last repose.
But far beyond, the phantom line
 In silence holds the dim parade,
Where radiant suns forever shine,
 "Across the river in the shade."

---

NOTE.—Among the bravest and best that ever shouldered a musket for the cause of Dixie, was the author's friend, comrade, and confident, Alonzo P. Hope, of Company A, Third Regiment, who, although wounded in the hip at Corinth, continued at his post, rejecting all tenders of a discharge from the service until the end. Mr. Hope now resides near Marshall, Texas, upon his farm, respected by all who know him.

# CHAPTER VII.

While encamped at Tupelo, the following orders were issued, relative to the remounting of the Texas Brigade:

"HEAD-QUARTERS, DISTRICT OF THE TENNESSEE,
"TUPELO, MISSISSIPPI, August 23d, 1862.
"Special Orders, No. 19—*Extract*.

"Brigadier-General Little will detail two commissioned officers and three men of the Third Texas Cavalry (dismounted), Colonel Mabry commanding, to bring from beyond the Mississippi river, the horses belonging to that regiment.

"By Order of MAJOR-GENERAL PRICE.
"JAMES M. LOUGHBOROUGH, A. A. G."

"FIRST DIVISION, DISTRICT OF THE TENNESSEE,
"HEAD-QUARTERS, POST AT SALTILLO, MISSISSIPPI, August, 1862.
"Special Order, No. 16.

"Captain J. N. Coleman, A. C. S.; First Lieutenant Logan, Company K; Sergeant-Major W. H. Gee, private Robert I. Haywood, Company G; and private J. D. Davis, Company E, are hereby detailed to bring from beyond the Mississippi river the horses and men belonging to the Third Texas Cavalry.

"By Order of BRIGADIER-GENERAL LITTLE.
"W. C. SHAMBURG, A. A. G."

"HEAD-QUARTERS, THIRD TEXAS CAVALRY,
CAMP NEAR SALTILLO, MISSISSIPPI, August 23d, 1862.
"Special Order, No. 1.

"The men belonging to this command, who were detailed under order No. —, issued by Major-General Van Dorn, Des Arc, Arkansas, April, 1862, to carry the horses belonging to this command to Texas,

GENERAL JOHN S. GRIFFITH.

are required to report to Captain John N. Coleman, at Marshall, Texas, for duty.

"H. P. MABRY, *Colonel, Commanding Third Texas.*

"Captain Coleman will receive recruits for the various companies as follows:

"Company A, Captain A. B. Stone, five men.
"Company B, Captain J. W. Wynne, five men.
"Company C, Captain J. A. Jones, twenty men.
"Company D, Captain R. S. Dabney, twenty-two men.
"Company E, Captain P. B. Ward, fourteen men.
"Company F, Captain R. F. Dunn, nine men.
"Company G, Captain E. S. Noble, ten men."

At Lumpkin's Mills, another brief halt was obtained, and while here the Texans, who were brigaded together at Holly Springs, learned of the arrival of the anxiously-expected horses. Alexander Selkirk hailed not with greater joy the first glimpse of the white sails that were to bear him from solitude, than did these men hail the arrival of their horses. It was announced that the horses were but a few miles distant. Orders arrived to prepare for another retreat; retreat had become a word nauseous, and the men were actually ashamed to retreat further. Brigades, divisions, *corps* passed the Texan camp. They had concluded, after consultation, not to march without their horses. When the drums beat to "fall in," the sound was absolutely drowned by the deafening cries, "HORSES!" "HORSES!" General Whitfield, the brigade commander, made them an appeal to duty, but the boys knew that "Old Whit" wished them mounted, and, at all events, that he "was with them" in any thing short of desertion. General Maury now appeared, and appealed to the men to proceed. Their sole reply was "HORSES!" "HORSES!" In despair the General turned away, and rode to overtake his retreating division.

Colonel Griffith, who was, at the time, in command of the Sixth Texas regiment, had his regiment called into line, and, after a calm review of the military situation, he showed how necessary it was for the maintenance of discipline; how infectious and fatal insubordination would prove, and appealed to the men not to tarnish their own honor, and place a bar sinister upon the escutcheon of Texas. He promised them that they should be mounted soon, and without the loss of honor, and concluded by inviting all who were disposed to remain at the post of duty, to return to their camp and prepare for the march. All responded but one solitary individual. To him, Griffith said: "Go, sir, and obey orders, or I will run you through with my saber!"

The effect of Griffith's appeal had the influence necessary to lead all the other regiments into the performance of duty, and saved them the lasting disgrace that such mutinous conduct, if persisted in, was sure to attach to their names. Heretofore, he had led them to victory over their enemies; he had, in this instance, led them to triumph over their baser passions; and the moralist would not hesitate to say that the latter was the most splendid victory of the two. Happily, the old brigade was never afterwards pervaded by so mean a spirit.

Similar orders to the foregoing were issued in regard to the other regiments of the Texas Brigade; but, like much other data referring to this work, was inaccessible to the author. This is regretted, and was sought to be obviated, by every effort that promised the slightest success, but only to be met with defeat.

Footworn and weary, the defeated army took up the line of retreat from Holly Springs, for what point they knew not, for it was but too apparent that General Grant could drive the Army of West Tennessee into the Gulf, if he so wished. Never did the Confederate Cross trail in the dust as at this time. The army was demoralized by the crushing defeat at Corinth; a defeat that burst upon them like a cyclone from a cloudless sky, in the very moment of victory. General Price took up the line of march from Abbeville to Grenada, as soon as it was evident that General Grant intended another advance. General Van Dorn had already made Oxford his head-quarters. Just before Price evacuated Abbeville, Colonel Griffith, in command of the Texas brigade, occupied the left wing, which rested on the Tallahatchie, near Toby Tuby ferry. This energetic and restless officer kept a vigilant watch on the enemy's movements, and, discovering a detached column of some five hundred cavalry, on the extreme right of the Federal position, asked and obtained permission of General Van Dorn to attack them. Returning to his command, Griffith caused forty rounds of ammunition to be issued to each man, and, after completing other necessary arrangements, was in the act of crossing the river, when orders arrived from General Van Dorn, countermanding the previous one, and directing Colonel Griffith to proceed down the Tallahatchie, via Panola, cross the Tokona, and thus place himself in the rear of General Washburne, who, at the head of an unknown force, was threatening Grenada, with a view of intercepting General Price's retreat. General Van Dorn's directions were for Griffith to harrass Washburne, by unexpected attacks upon his rear, and thus retard his movements, until General Price could bring off his large wagon-train, wounded, artillery, etc. With his usual energy, Griffith made the necessary dispositions for the care of his wagon-train, and, within an hour, was ready to set out upon this unexpected expedition. The Brigade consisted of the Legion, Third and Sixth Texas Cavalry, and Captain McNally's battery of four guns. After a forced march to the Tokona, it was discovered that all the fords were strongly guarded, and that it would be impossible to penetrate the enemy's rear. In this dilemma, Griffith boldly determined to throw his little brigade in Washburne's immediate front, and risk the safety of Price's retreat upon the issue. The odds were terrible, but he argued that if his brigade was cut to pieces, that the salvation of the army would have been purchased cheaply enough—a disinterested decision, worthy a hero. In pursuance of this resolution, he proceeded up the Tokona, and hastily communicated this decision to General Van Dorn, who immediately replied, in the following brief dispatch, which, however, gave Colonel Griffith full authority to act as he should elect:

"HEAD-QUARTERS,
"DEPARTMENT OF MISSISSIPPI AND EAST LOUISIANA,
"OXFORD, MISSISSIPPI, December 1st, 1862.

"*Colonel Griffith*: I am directed by the General commanding, to say, that if you carry out what you propose, it will be what he desires. He has no instructions to give. The army has now fallen back, and will be to-night on the Tokona.
"I am, respectfully,
"R. W. MEMMINGER, A. A. G."

But the readiness of Griffith to assume grave responsibilities, when he deemed that the interest of the cause was to be subserved thereby, as exemplified in his charge, contrary to orders, at Chustenahlah, now asserted itself, and he was deep into the practical execution already of his project to strike Washburne in front, when the above dispatch reached him. The Tokona was passed, and the head of the column was nearing the enemy, in the neighborhood of Oakland. From a few stragglers from the enemy's ranks, it was learned that General Washburne was in command of eight or ten thousand infantry, and about two thousand cavalry. Griffith's brigade numbered not more than twelve hundred effective men. It was a bold stroke, conceived by the daring Texan, but demanded by the exigencies of the occasion. In consequence of the rapidity of the march, the battery was left in the care of a number of the men whose horses were too jaded to proceed. On the night of the second, learning that the enemy's cavalry were occupying Preston, the irrepressible ranger dashed into that place, but only to discover that the "blue-coats" had retired to Mitchell's Cross Roads, on hearing of the arrival of the Confederate cavalry at Grenada.

On the morning of the third, learning that Washburne, at the head of his whole force, was moving on the town of Oakland, Griffith immediately determined to meet him at the junction of the road he was marching upon with the Charleston road, and a half mile beyond town. Colonel Boggess, of the Third, was directed to make a demonstration on his left and rear; Captain Jack Wharton, commanding the Sixth, took position on the Charleston road; Colonel Hawkins, commanding the Legion, together with Major J. H. Broocks, temporarily commanding three detached companies, constituted the center. Major Broocks, being in the advance, speedily opened the engagement by a vigorous attack, which was met by the enemy with a spirited return. Colonel E. R. Hawkins dismounted his men under the cover of a slight natural elevation, and moved up in excellent order on the right of Broocks.\* The battle was now general, and the gallant Hawkins, and the veteran Legion, maintained their position against a force outnumbering them in the ratio of ten to one. The artillery of the enemy literally poured into their devoted ranks grape and canister with a rapidity and pre-

---

\* At the battle of Oakland, Sergeant Cellum, of the Third Texas, at the head of thirty men, penetrated the enemy's rear, and captured several wagons loaded with commissary supplies, killing several of the guard, and making some twenty prisoners.

cision of aim rarely exceeded. Griffith, true to the boldness of his original conception, ordered a charge upon the battery, and the brave fellows, responding with a yell of triumph, irresistibly charged in the wake of their gallant leaders, and took the murder-dealing guns; and, without a moment to re-form their disordered line, attacked, and drove from the field, the infantry that was supporting the battery. The enemy now planted another battery on their right, and opened a cross-fire upon the Legion. Colonel Griffith ordered Captain Wharton to dismount his men, and take the battery. The brave Wharton was eagerly complying with this order, when intelligence reached Colonel Griffith that the enemy was outflanking his left. The Texans were immediately summoned to horse, as the safety of the command demanded a speedy withdrawal from the enfolding lines of the enemy's superior numbers. This delicate maneuver was performed, under fire, in perfect order, and line of battle re-formed in the suburbs of Oakland. The spirited engagement had continued fifty minutes, and the loss on the side of the enemy was considerable. The Texans lost ten men. General Washburne did not wish another repetition of the dose, and, with the friendly cover of the night, retired to the crossroads.

This engagement, small in itself, was of vital consequence to the army of Price, in that it drove from its rear an army of 12,000 Federals. General Washburne evidently imagined that he was confronted by a division of Van Dorn's army, for had he known the inconsiderable number of his assailants, it is not probable that he would have turned his back to them. The boldness and spirit of Griffith's attack was sufficient data upon which to predicate such a hypothesis. Of course, during the presence of Washburne's force in the rear of General Price, the trains on the railroad had ceased to run. Colonel Griffith immediately forwarded to General Price some fifteen trains, with which to facilitate his retreat. Thanks to the boldness of the victors at Oakland, the brave old Missourian was enabled to save all his stores, and reached Grenada, on the south of the Yallabusha river, in due course.

The distracted and suffering army of West Tennessee was now allowed a respite from the alarums of battle; but how long it would continue, no one presumed to know; all feared that the victorious Grant would soon push onward. General Van Dorn was, at this time, superseded in the command of the army by Lieutenant-General J. C. Pemberton. Of the organization of a cavalry corps, to be commanded by General Van Dorn, and the conception of the Holly Springs expedition, *vide* "Biography of General Griffith," in this volume.

The army of General Pemberton, numbering about 25,000 illy-disciplined, poorly-clothed and fed men, occupied the town and vicinity of Grenada. General U. S. Grant was in command of 75,000 disciplined, and thoroughly-supplied and equipped men, accustomed to victory, and occupied the town of Coffeeville. Memphis was General Grant's base of operations, and Holly Springs an intermediate depot, where had been accumulated immense stores of supplies and munitions of war. This latter place was garrisoned by about 2,500 men. In compliance with orders from General Pemberton, Colonel Griffith reported to General Van Dorn for duty, with his brigade, on December 12, 1862, composed and officered as follows:

> Ninth Texas Cavalry—Colonel D. W. Jones, commanding.
> Third Texas Cavalry—Lieutenant-Colonel J. S. Boggess, commanding.
> Sixth Texas Cavalry—Captain Jack Wharton, commanding.
> First Texas Legion Calvary—Major J. H. Broocks, commanding.

In addition to the Texas Brigade, General Van Dorn's command comprised the brigade of General W. H. Jackson, composed of Tennessee and Mississippi cavalry, and the Missouri Brigade of Colonel McCulloch, the whole aggregating about 3,500 men. The object and purposes of the expedition were enveloped in absolute secrecy, and Van Dorn set out from Grenada, it is believed, on the night of December 19, and pursued the hasty march all night and the next day.

Passing through the beautiful town of Pontotoc, the hungry troopers were enthusiastically welcomed by the noble and patriotic citizens of the place; and trays, dishes, and baskets of the choicest edibles were offered on all sides, and pitchers of wine and milk as well. No halt was allowed, and the men pursued their mysterious way munching the welcomed "grub" dispensed by the fair hands of Pontotoc's good, and beautiful, and noble heroines. O, peerless ladies of Pontotoc, though the mists of twenty years becloud the mind's eye, and interminable leagues intervene between us, the courtly Griffith, and his surviving "rebels," salute you! You who were radiant maidens, then, and had, perchance, plighted your vows with those of a soldier lover, are matrons now. Time despoils the cheek of its damask, but the heart, like old wine, grows the better from the effects of age. May your clime continue to produce a type of womanhood as noble and exalted as your own; for emulation will find, at the standard of your excellence, an *ultima thule* beyond which there can be no progression!

General Van Dorn had dispatched a trusty spy, well acquainted with the place, to Holly Springs, to ascertain the number and position of the enemy, and to accurately locate the picket on the Ripley road. The command proceeded at a brisk pace, in a northerly direction, and crossed the Holly Springs road three miles north of the Ripley road. Here the Federal scouts, hitherto hanging on the Confederate rear, returned to their camp, satisfied that having passed Holly Springs so far to the left, that the object of the rebel raid was to be found in Tennessee. The command halted at 3 P.M., on the 21st, and the men regaled themselves on broiled pork and luscious sweet potatoes.

General Van Dorn summoned Colonel Griffith to his presence, and imparted to him the plan of the purposed attack. The spy returned with accurate data as to all necessary information, and further stated that the Yankees, apprehending no danger, were preparing for a grand ball. The command was disposed of as follows: Jackson's Brigade on the right, Griffith's the center, and McCulloch's the left. At nightfall, Van Dorn counter-marched, and proceeded back to the Ripley and Holly Springs road, and thence to Holly Springs, moving by columns of fours, and guns uncapped. Silently, Jackson leads his brigade to the right, and McCulloch his to the left, and the meshes of fate are encircling the unconscious Federals.

Guards had been left at all the houses in the immediate vicinity of the line of march, and other precautions taken to prevent the possibility of the intelligence of Van Dorn's return passing into the city. Slowly and cautiously, the command moves along through the darkness, like some monster serpent, conscious of its ability to seize and crush its prey. Lieutenant Hyams, of General Van Dorn's staff, was dispatched on the delicate mission to capture the picket, without the discharge of a gun, for one pistol-shot would apprise the slumbering Federals of the presence of their enemy. That the mission of this young officer was an entire success, speaks volumes in praise of his bravery, coolness, and sagacity. The enterprise contained the elements of ninety-nine failures to one of success. General Van Dorn directed Colonel Griffith to charge at the head of the Sixth and Ninth into the town. "And take care," added the General, "that you do not find a hornet's-nest at the square!" With drawn saber, Griffith places himself at the head of the charging column. "Forward, at a gallop!" he commands, and the squadrons move down the road; and, as the suburbs are reached, the bugle's shrill, harsh blast sounds the charge upon the crisp morning air, and shouting, yelling rebels disturb the slumbers of Federal soldiers and citizens, alike. The former emerge from their tents to be informed that they are prisoners of war; and the latter—mostly women and children—to shout: "Hurrah for Van Dorn! Hurrah for the Confederacy!! Hurrah for Jeff. Davis!!!" Little children bring forth miniature Confederate flags that they have been forced to conceal since the "Yankees" came; beautiful young ladies wave their handkerchiefs, and matrons implore the protection of God for the charging soldiers. Tears of joy gush forth from many an eye, and manly voices grow husky from emotion. O, that entry into Holly Springs was the incident of a life-time!

Colonel Griffith posted the Third, under Colonel Boggess, in the square, and detailed the Legion, at the instance of General Van Dorn, to guard the prisoners. Colonel Broocks faithfully performed this duty, as indeed he always did, and kept his men well in hand, and none of the Legion engaged in the subsequent plundering of the stores that ensued. Colonel Broocks had four men detailed from each company at a time, and, in a decent manner, these procured whatever they wished of the captured property. This conscientious officer allowed no prisoner to be robbed of his individual property, and, while he thus honored himself and his State, kept the bright escutcheon of the Confederacy untarnished. A regiment of Iowa troops were seen forming line just out of town, and Colonel Griffith ordered Colonel Jones to form his regiment—the Ninth—so as to charge them down the street. A flag of truce was now raised in a camp to the left, and Griffith dispatched an aid to receive the surrender; in the meantime, placing himself by the side of the gallant "boy colonel," Jones, they lead the Ninth in a headlong charge against the Iowa warriors; disperse them, take their colors, and many prisoners.

Colonel Griffith now dispatched to General Van Dorn: "The 'hornet's-nest' is ours!" and joined Colonel Boggess in the square.

Many ladies—some still in *dishabille*—throng the square; all rejoicing, all excited, and none looking to future consequences. They point out to Griffith the house occupied by Mrs. Grant, the paymaster, and the chief quartermaster. Colonel Griffith sent guards to arrest all the officers domiciled in houses, and to the house occupied by Mrs. Grant, at which were several of the General's staff. Griffith detailed ten men, in the special charge of Colonel Boggess, as a guarantee that the ladies should be treated with deference and respect. But a few minutes elapsed when a messenger from Boggess announced to Colonel Griffith that three ladies denied him entrance to the house. Griffith, fearing some rudeness might be committed, repaired to the scene immediately, when Colonel Boggess exclaimed: "I can not execute your orders without the exercise of violence to these ladies!" Mrs. Grant, stepping forward, said: "And you, sir, make war upon women, do you?" "On the contrary, madam," replied the knightly Griffith, doffing his plumed chapeau, and bowing profoundly to the lady; "we leave that to our enemies!" But the ladies continued to "hold the fort," and Griffith, addressing the soldiers, said: "Men, offer no rudeness to the ladies; if they will not allow you to pass through the gate, tear off a picket from the fence, and flank them; if you are denied admittance at the door, go around them, and find ingress through a window. You must search the house for concealed prisoners, but do not touch the hem of the garment of one of these ladies." The men commenced tearing off the pickets to the right and left of the gate, when Mrs. Grant relented, and politely invited them to enter through the gate, at the same time protesting that there were no men in the house. One officer was found in the house. Colonel Griffith placed a guard over the house, for the protection of the ladies, while the command remained in town.

McCulloch's Brigade now arrived at the square, and some of the men broke into a sutler's store, and commenced an indiscriminate pillage. Colonel Griffith, knowing that the infection would become contagious, appealed to the men, in the absence of their officers, to desist. His appeals to the Missourians were, however, futile; and soon Tennesseeans, Mississippians, and Texans, vied in the work of pillage; the latter *nationality*, however, always keeping a sharp look out for their commander. Of course, all this was wrong, was destructive of discipline, and would have proved fatal in its consequences had a few hundred Federal troopers dashed into town; but the poor, ragged, half-starved fellows, deserved all they got, and more. Never did an army undergo as complete a transformation, in external appearances, in so short a time. The grimy, ragged rebel of a moment ago, now appears with the uniform-coat of a Federal colonel on his back, a plumed hat on his head, and his feet and legs are encased in patent-leather cavalry-boots. *In vino veritas!* at least one would have imagined as much to judge from the frequent and liberal potations indulged in by, alas! too many. Cigars were plentiful, and about three thousand of them were kept puffing at a time. The property captured and destroyed was estimated at over $5,000,000 worth. Besides the stores that were filled with the goods of the sutlers and the government, immense quantities of bacon, pork, flour in sacks, hard bread, coffee, etc., etc., were stacked in piles as high as a man's head, and in rows a quarter of a mile long, at the depot. Great quantities of arms and ammunition were found. The court-house was the magazine, and contained an immense quantity of ordnance stores, bomb-shells, powder, etc. This was fired as the command left the city, and the exploding pieces sounded, at a distance, as if a battle was in progress.

The dream of John S. Griffith was realized—the blow had been struck, and it only remained to be seen what effect it would have in causing the great Federal captain to change his plans for the reduction of Vicksburg.

As the fifth act of the drama, in this connection, does not properly pertain to our narrative, it will only be remarked, *en passant*, that the result was all that had been hoped for. General Grant withdrew his forces from that front, to Memphis, and inaugurated his celebrated movement down the Mississippi river, directly against Vicksburg, and the Texas Brigade was summoned, from the mountains of distant Tennessee, to attend the obsequies of the Army of West Tennessee, on July 4, 1863.

The following incidents attracted the attention of the author during the brief sojourn of the distinguished Southern party at the headquarters of General Grant. Our fortunes had undergone such remarkable changes in the last few hours, that nothing now could possibly surprise us. We had stepped from privation to plenty, and many were disposed to inaugurate a jubilee, inspired by the spirit of John Barleycorn, Esq.

Here comes Pennington, of the Third, with $20,000 in crisp, new greenbacks that he has discovered. He'd dispose of the batch for five dollars in silver. Despairing of drinking all the whisky, and having engagements elsewhere, the rebels knock the heads of the whisky-barrels in, and the streets of Holly Springs, literally, are flooded with whisky. A big, red-headed Irishman, in his shirt-sleeves, but wearing a Federal officer's trowsers, called Colonel Mulligan—whether derisively or not, *quien sabe?*—takes advantag eof the sudden decline in liquors, and drinks confusion to his enemies with the pillaged whisky of his friends. "Ye coom like thaves in the dark!" cries the melo-dramatic Colonel Mulligan. "Is this the way to make warr on a civilized people? But ye'll nivir, no nivir, escape!" "Release the prisoners in the jail," is the next order. We find many Federal soldiers incarcerated, some of whom join the ranks of their liberators. Many citizens imprisoned without a charge being preferred against them. But, shade of Brian Boru! who have we here else than Mr. B. Thomas! O, inimitable son of the Emerald Isle! My old comrade, whose loyal friendship was as true as steel, and whose aversion for guard duty was stronger than his hatred of the devil, what fate hath befallen thee since we parted so long ago under the "Stars and Bars?" Mr. Thomas informs us that he is under sentence of death as a spy. "And if ye hadn't a come, it was shooting me they would the day afther the morrow. I'm glad to see yez, boys, and glad yez canteens are full."

> "O, I am not fond of wurruck,
> It was nivir the gift of the Bradies,
> But sure I'd make a most illegant Turruck,
> For I'm fond of tobaccy and ladies!"

Mr. Thomas did not exaggerate his case a particle. He was discharged from the Third Texas after the conclusion of the first year's service, as being over the age of re-enlistment; whereupon, he engaged in the business of a sutler to the regiment. In quest of necessaries for his shop, Mr. Thomas ventured into the enemy's lines as affording a more varied market from which to select his purchases, with the result already remarked.

Colonel Griffith, as elsewhere stated, commanded the "Texas Brigade" in this, perhaps, most remarkable campaign of the war, and was second to no officer, in the *corps*, in contributing to its unparalleled success. He charged at the head of the Texans into the city, and his black plume waved in the thickest of the fight at Middleburg and Davis' Mill. Cool in the hottest fever of battle, he was brave even unto rashness. But happily, his temerity and impetuosity were held in subjection by a sagacious intelligence, and prudence characterized all his actions. General Griffith is no less a gentleman of letters and culture, than of action on the field, and he would grace any civil position in the State—that he would consent to occupy—with profit to the people and honor to the office. His friend, the author, looks forward to his civil preferment with happy anticipations; knowing, full well, that Texas has no truer son upon whom she could confer her honors in part compensation for the arduous services that he has rendered her, on distant fields, which made the Texan name glorious.

Upon the immediate capture of Holly Springs, an indescribable scene of pillage ensued. In some commands, soldiers no longer recognized their officers, and, apparently, all subordination and discipline were lost sight of. It was, doubtless, a diverting scene to the prisoners, who longed in their hearts to see a few hundred of their blue-coated comrades come charging into town, and route the greedy rebels who were sacking it. And, in truth, this would not have been impossible, had the evil continued unchecked. But seeing some of his own brigade catching the disgraceful infection, Colonel Griffith appealed to them to remain at their posts of duty, and not disgrace the fair fame of the Confederacy by such riotous conduct. But some of the men not heeding the soldierly appeal to their noble natures, the determined chieftain drew his sword, and, in language more forcible than polite, vowed that he would constitute himself the custodian of Confederate honor, and drove the delinquents, at its point, back into the ranks.

The Texans bore the brunt of each engagement on this expedition. Wherever opposition was encountered, the gallant Griffith led his Texans through the revel of death, and wherever the conflict deepened most, his sable plume, like the oriflamme of Henry of Navarre, was seen. To the sterling soldierly qualities of Colonel John S. Griffith, was the Confederate cause indebted, in no small degree, for this success, which, in its results, exceeded those of many of the most stubbornly-contested battles of the war.

The prisoners captured in Holly Springs numbered between 2,800 and 3,000. But of infinitely more value than the paroling of these, or the destruction of the vast accumulation of supplies, was the rendering of Holly Springs a strategic point of no further importance in the "Great Captain's" campaign against Vicksburg.

About four o'clock in the afternoon, and as soon as the work of paroling the prisoners was accomplished, the command resumed the march northward. Nothing occurred, worthy of mention, until the fortified position of "Davis' Mill" was reached, just beyond the Tennessee line. Here a force of some three or four hundred Federals were ensconced in a palisade fort, having an impassable stream in its front, across which the assailants must move over a foot-bridge, exposed to the fire from the fort. A curious contrivance, employed here, was a cannon mounted on a hand-car, which, from the facility with which it could be shifted from position to position, caused the Confederates considerable injury and annoyance. The Texas Brigade was dismounted, and marched to the attack in fine spirits, led by the intrepid Griffith. Colonel Griffith ordered Colonel Broocks, with the Legion, to cross the stream above the bridge on some logs, and assail the position in flank. This movement the gallant Broocks executed in excellent order, and had General Van Dorn not called Griffith from the attack in front, to resume the march into Tennessee, the place must inevitably have been taken by the Confederates. The engagement was warm, and the Texans left about twenty dead upon the field, and twice that number wounded. At the bridge, in going to the attack, and in retreating from the field, volley after volley was poured into their ranks, wholly exposed to the enemy's aim, as they defiled across the narrow causeway, and deployed into line on the other side of the stream. The engagement continued, without intermission, for about three hours, when General Van Dorn, seeing the futility of his attacks on the fortified position without guns, called off the men. Again must the gauntlet be run at the fatal bridge, and again did the vigilant enemy improve the occasion by a free use of their rifles. A Confederate hospital was erected on the field, and left in charge of Assistant-Surgeon Eugene Blocker, of the Third Texas.

Northward, again, the indefatigable Van Dorn led the march, and, in the afternoon of the next day, came in the neighborhood of Bolivar, Tennessee, at which place was a considerable force of the enemy. General Van Dorn amused them by a skirmish with the Tennesseeans and Mississippians, while the Texans attacked a strongly-fortified position at Middleburg, a few miles distant. One prominent feature of this position was a block-house, absolutely impregnable to attacks by small arms. The position was stormed again and again, but no foothold could be gained, and General Van Dorn, despairing of success, abandoned the undertaking late in the afternoon.

The author omitted to state, in its proper connection, that the railroad track was torn up at various points between Holly Springs and Bolivar, and the telegraph wires cut. The object of the expedition was now attained, and the column turned to retrace its way by a circuitous route. The Federal cavalry were making superhuman efforts to capture Van Dorn, and endeavoring to intercept the column—a force of cavalry and mounted infantry, not far short of 10,000 men, were employed. Frequent skirmishes were had with this force on the return, the last of which occurred at Ripley, Mississippi.

The month of January was passed by the Texas Brigade in doing picket duty, and in scouting expeditions in and about Water Valley. There being no longer any immediate need of cavalry in Mississippi, the command of General Van Dorn was ordered to Tennessee. Before commencing the long and fatiguing march, Van Dorn issued his celebrated "Order No. 5," in which he prescribed the minutest rules for the government of his *corps*, whether in camp or on the march. Proper distances were prescribed to be observed on the march between companies, regiments, brigades, and divisions; a regular system of bugle calls was formulated; challenges and replies of videttes, etc., etc.—the whole concluding with the impetuous declaration: "Cavalry knows no danger—knows no failure; *what it is ordered to do, it must do!*" The seemingly interminable march to Tennessee was wearisome in the extreme, and utterly devoid of interesting incident. The army of General Bragg was encamped at Tullahoma and Shelbyville. His left flank was threatened by a force of about 10,000 men, under General Granger, at Franklin. The object of Van Dorn was to confront this force, and prevent, if possible, its further advance in the direction of Duck river. This stream was crossed over a pontoon-bridge at Columbia, and the column proceeded to Spring Hill, on the pike connecting Columbia and Franklin. Several skirmishes were had with the enemy in the neighborhood of Franklin; when, finally, about March 5, 1863, General

COLONEL JACK WHARTON.

Granger determined to put a period to Van Dorn's annoyances, and, affecting to despise the prowess of his adversary, dispatched Colonel Coburn, with 3,000 infantry, a battery of artillery, and about 500 cavalry, to drive the audacious rebel across Duck river. Van Dorn met the expeditionary column at Thompson's Station, near Spring Hill; and, while engaging him in front with the Texas Brigade, dispatched General Forrest—who had reported to him for duty—to gain the enemy's rear. The Texans made charge after charge, upon the line of the enemy, and the author would bear witness to the bravery and soldierly bearing of Colonel Coburn, who fought with a valor worthy of a better issue. Outnumbered, surrounded, and being attacked by the impetuous charges of the Texans every moment, he finally raised the white flag, and surrendered to General Van Dorn in front of the Texas Brigade. The prisoners surrendered were about 3,000, as the cavalry and artillery escaped. Again, the author regrets that he is unable to present any thing like an accurate estimate of the Confederate loss. A comrade of the author, in a late letter, says: "I think all the estimates place the loss of the Texas Brigade too low. The Legion carried into the battle 225 men, after leaving one-fourth of the whole to hold the horses; and, my recollection is, that the killed and wounded of the Legion numbered seventy-five. Company E came out of the fight with only half its number (twenty-eight), unhurt. Those true gentlemen and splendid officers, Captain B. H. Norsworthy (afterward promoted Major), and Lieutenant Lipscomb Norvell, being of the severely wounded. That victory was indeed dearly bought by our brigade, no matter from what other quarter attempts have been made to appropriate the honors of it. With feelings of mingled pride and sadness, I continually, in my mind, look back upon the scenes of that day, and hear voices that are no longer of this world. Captain J. W. Bazer, commanding Company H of the Legion, with kindness of heart, intelligence, and iron nerve stamped on his countenance, severely wounded, but continuing duty on the field until shot dead."

Lieutenant Alley, of Company G of the Legion, always the gentleman and soldier, in fact and bearing, his black plume waving in the thickest of the fight until mortally wounded. Captain James A. Broocks, commanding Company C of the Legion, with his clear, ringing voice: "Come on, Company C!" The author would bear testimony to the daring and chivalry of Captain Broocks, who, upon that occasion, seemed to court the missions of danger like a Saladin bearing a charmed life. But he was struck down in his ripe manhood. To Colonel John H. Broocks, his brother, the dying patriot said: "John, take this sword (their venerable father had given it to him), and tell father that I died in the performance of my duty." Noble words—example worthy the emulation of Southern youth for all time! Lieutenant C. H. Roberts, Company C of the Legion, true and brave, was killed at the head of his company. Privates Spoon, Elezer Davis, and John Bryant, of the Legion, and Drew Polk, and David B. Nicholson, of Company E, Third Texas Regiment, always distinguished for soldierly qualities, were all slain in close propinquity. The engagement continued, without intermission, about five hours; and, so deadly and stubborn was the nature of the contest, that at times bayonets actually clashed, and hand to hand fights to the death were not uncommon. Here fell one of nature's noblemen—Wyndham, First Sergeant of Company A, Third Texas. In the morning of manhood, he left his Louisiana home, and came to tender his services, and his life, to the cause of the South. Pure in his character, of a high and lofty nature, and talents far above mediocrity, Wyndham was justly regarded by his friends as a young man of great promise. Alas, what fond, proud hopes went down with him! He sleeps all alone, far from the home and friends of his youth, without a slab of marble to mark the spot; but he lives in the hearts of all who knew him,

> "For none knew him but to love,
> None named him but to praise!"

If the capture of Holly Springs was the most important cavalry exploit of the war, the battle of Thompson's Station was not by any means the least. As an effort has been made to detract from the hard-earned fame of the Texas Brigade on this occasion, the author refers to a "defense" published in the Waco *Examiner and Patron*, and which has been endorsed by a number of officers of the Texas Brigade as being correct and just in all particulars, save that the loss in killed and wounded is underestimated.

Though not exactly in its proper connection, the original organization of Whitfield's Legion will be given here, together with a statement of its participation in the battle of Iuka. As this data came anonymously by mail, the author does not know to whom his thanks are due for the same: "Whitfield's Legion was organized April 2, 1862, by the addition of nine new companies to Whitfield's Battalion, the companies of the old battalion, to-wit: A, Captain E. R. Hawkins; B, Captain Murphy; C, Captain John H. Broocks; and D, Captain John T. Whitfield, carrying with them into the Legion the same letter designations respectively, that they had in the battalion. Major J. W. Whitfield was elected Colonel without opposition. The organization was not completed until April 19, when Captain E. R. Hawkins was elected Lieutenant-Colonel, and Private S. Holman, Major. The command was composed of eleven companies from Texas and two from Arkansas, up to, and a short time after, the re-organization, when the Arkansas Company B—Captain W. Catterson—was transferred to an Arkansas command. At the 're-organization' (May 8, 1862), all the field-officers were re-elected, and the companies were commanded by the following officers: A, Captain J. N. Zackry; B, Captain W. Catterson (vice Captain Murphy); C, Captain John H. Broocks; D, Captain John T. Whitfield; E, Captain B. H. Norsworthy; F, Captain Ben. Griffin; G, Captain Ed. O. Williams; H, Captain —————; I, Captain Jesse M. Cook; K, Captain —————; L, Captain ————; M, Captain O. P. Preston; N, Captain —————. Major Holman resigned, and Captain John H. Broocks was promoted in his stead. On May 9, 1863, Colonel Whitfield was appointed Brigadier-General, after which, Lieutenant-Colonel Hawkins was promoted Colonel, Major Brooks, Lieutenant-Colonel, and Captain John T. Whitfield, Major.

"On September 19, 1862, the Legion participated in the Battle of Iuka. It occupied the position on the right of the brigade. When the skirmishers were driven back, Colonel Whitfield ordered a charge. The Third Texas, which had been thrown forward as skirmishers, seeing us advance, fell into ranks with us, and thus formed—as one regiment—we captured the Ninth Ohio Battery, driving the enemy before us. The Forty-second Iowa attempted to make a right-wheel, so as to enfilade the line, but three companies, and about seventy men of the Third Texas, charged, and drove it in confusion from the field. In this engagement, the three Cook brothers, of the Legion, greatly distinguished themselves for cool intrepidity and loyal devotion to the flag of the Confederacy. Ensign Ivey Cook was shot down, severely wounded, when his brother, Samuel, seized the regimental colors, and waved them with a cheer of triumph. But he advanced but a few steps, when he, too, was shot down; when a third brother, young Andrew Cook, grasped the staff from his relaxing hold, exclaiming: 'The flag shall wave, though the entire Cook family is exterminated in the attempt!' Colonel Whitfield was severely wounded. The loss of the regiment was 107 killed and wounded. On October 5, 1862, the Legion participated in the engagement at Hatchie Bridge, while the battle of Corinth was in progress. We were first formed on the north bank of the river; were then moved to the south bank, and formed in line, with the river in our rear. We were attacked by an overwhelming force and driven back. Our loss was very great in prisoners, as the bridge was torn in pieces by the enemy's shell, and the means of passing the stream was difficult and dangerous. Our loss, during the engagement, was ninety-seven in killed, wounded, and prisoners."

The author regrets that he does not know to whom he is indebted for the above extract; but, knowing the general correctness of the statements given, he has no hesitation whatever in embodying it in the narrative of the services of the Texas Brigade.

### A TEXAN'S ESTIMATE OF GENERAL W. S. HANCOCK, U. S. A.

#### I.

Hancock, the smiling Muse lights on thy name,
With stylus ready to record thy fame;
The legend reads upon the tablet traced—
In letters that may never be effaced.

#### II.

In war the superb soldier's matchless blade,
Gleamed first and last along the lines array'd;
When Peace arose with crown of olive wreath,
His tempered steel was first to seek its sheath.

#### III.

Though others in the drama bore conspicuous part,
*He* won the fortress of his foeman's heart;
The civic chief, by all the sections blest,
Who knew no North, no South, no East, no West!

---

NOTE.—During the march of the 20th, Colonel Griffith galloped to the head of the column, and rode with General Van Dorn an hour or more. Griffith represented to the General that, inasmuch as he was the originator of the expedition, he should be granted the post of honor; or, in other words, bear the brunt of the fighting; that his regiments, having served as infantry, would be more efficient than those drilled purely as cavalry. General Van Dorn readily acquiesced, and took occasion to thank the Colonel for having, in such complimentary terms, suggested himself as the commander. He also complimented Colonel Griffith on the conception of such a bold *ruse de guerre*, which promised such sterling results to the cause.

NOTE.—Upon the entry of the Confederates into Holly Springs, Colonel Griffith was informed that General U. S. Grant had just departed, on a special train, for Memphis; and the locomotive that bore the modern Cæsar and his fortunes, could even then be located by the smoke escaping from its chimney. A delay of five minutes, on his part, would have materially cheeked that tide in his affairs, that was bearing him on to fortune and to fame.

NOTE.—At the instance of Colonel Broocks, their regimental commander, honorable mention is made of the following officers and men of the " Legion," as their due for soldierly qualities exhibited on all occasions:

Lieutenant Thompson Morris, Company I, First Texas Legion.
Captain J. M. Cook, Company I, First Texas Legion.
T. M. Bagby, Company F, First Texas Legion.
Lieutenant Snell, Company F, First Texas Legion.
Sergeant M. McQuistain, Company G, First Texas Legion.
Captain Dave Snodgrass, illegally promoted from a lieutenancy in his own company, to the captaincy of another, by virtue of General Bragg's autocratic ukase of 1862.
John F. Pleasants, Company C, First Texas Legion.
Captain Adam Adams, Company E, First Texas Legion.
Captain Ed. O. Williams, Company G, First Texas Legion.
Lieutenant W. B. Walker, Company D, who lost an arm in the battles around Atlanta, while at the post of duty.
Rev. R. W. Thompson, the able and efficient Chaplain of the Legion.

The author cheerfully adds to these the names of Ulysses Hairgrove, Company K, Third Texas Cavalry, who was as brave as he was always willing and ready for battle. First Sergeant Thomas J. Cellum, Company A, Third Texas Cavalry, who was always at his post, and ready to take a hand in any thing that might turn up. Hays Alston, R. A. Godbold, Fannin Montgomery, and Jack Phillips, of the same company and regiment, recur to the mind; but, where all were actuated by motives the most disinterested and patriotic, it would seem invidious to make distinctions by the special mention of any.

# CHAPTER VIII.

After the battle of Thompson's Station, the brigade encamped near the village of Spring Hill, on the Columbia and Franklin pike, for a week or ten days—a respite from service of which both horses and men stood much in need. But General Granger finally moved down the pike with an overwhelming force. Van Dorn retired in the direction of Columbia, sullenly disputing every inch of ground. As the recent heavy rains had caused the streams to rise, and more rain threatened, General Van Dorn very sagaciously crossed the wagon-train and battery of artillery over the river. General Granger's force now occupied the position of a horseshoe, extending from the river on the right of Van Dorn, to the river on his left. The Confederates were enveloped in the folds of the anaconda-like enemy; and, to complete the picture of their seemingly wretched condition, the pontoon-bridge was swept away, leaving a swollen, roaring torrent in their rear. General Van Dorn recognized the desperation of the situation, and addressed himself at once to redeem it; and, on this occasion, he unquestionably showed those qualities of quick perception, rapid decision, and indomitable pluck, that characterizes the captain of genius. An attack, in force, was made on the enemy's extreme right, which forced him to draw re-enforcements from the left to come to the rescue of the threatened wing, thus leaving an outlet which the sagacious Van Dorn was not slow to improve. Placing himself at the head of the Third Texas Cavalry, the General led the way, followed by the remainder of the corps. Granger was surprised and chagrined to see his wily adversary elude his grasp, in what he, doubtless, deemed the moment of victory. Van Dorn took up the line of march for Shelbyville, and, crossing the river at that point, returned to Columbia. The pontoon was soon repaired, and the corps was, ere many days, in front of Franklin, to which post the discomforted Granger had retraced his steps. The brigade, while here, was engaged in doing very arduous picket duty, and in foraging almost under the guns of the enemy. Frequent skirmishes, and partial engagements, took place; though the redoubtable Granger did not again venture out of his stronghold. The Legion, while doing picket duty in an advanced and very exposed position, was surprised one night by the enemy, and suffered some loss.

While encamped here, the assassination of General Van Dorn occurred. This was one of the severest blows to the Confederacy. Cavalry, pre-eminently, was the arm upon which the South should have relied, as by rapidity of movement, the deficiency in numbers could, in a measure, have been obviated. Van Dorn, Stuart, and Forrest, with 10,000 well-mounted and well-armed men, would, undoubtedly, have accomplished great results. As we have seen, Van Dorn frustrated Grant's army of 75,000 men with barely 3,000 troopers, and the results of the capture of Holly Springs was just the same as if Pemberton had driven Grant to Memphis; and, in a humanitarian sense, much greater, since the butchery was avoided. Forrest, with 5,000 men, fell upon Smith and Grierson, and crushed them, though they had full 15,000 men. Had this column joined Sherman at Meridian, as doubtless was the intention, the Georgia campaign had never been, for Sherman would have marched to Mobile, and the end would have been.

The circumstances attending the killing of General Van Dorn belong to history, and the public have a right to demand the whole truth, and, whatever delicacy of feeling we may have in regard to invading the sacred precincts of the domestic circle, vanish, when circumstances have invited the inexorable stylus of history to secure a record in the case; yet the author has no relish for such episodes, and is glad that another has kindly performed most of the unpleasant duty of reciting the causes of the homicide, and so relieved him of a very uncongenial task. There were no witnesses to the unfortunate act. The writer was encamped within three hundred yards of the house at the time, and can but give the report as current then. The head-quarters of General Van Dorn were at the residence of Major Chairs, a few rods from the house of Dr. Peters. On the morning of the homicide, the General rose from the breakfast-table in advance of his staff, and proceeded, alone, to his office, where he found Dr. Peters waiting. The latter presented a pass to Franklin, to the General, for his signature. Van Dorn took the paper, sat down to the desk to sign it. Peters, standing behind him, awaited the final stroke of the pen, when he drew a Smith & Wesson revolver and fired, the ball entering the back of the head, and lodging just under the surface above the right eye. The assassin, licensed by the pass, mounted his horse, and a few minutes gallop passed him through the enemy's lines. Peters was subsequently apprehended, and tried in Mississippi before a Confederate court, and acquitted. The following account of his arrest, as given by Lieutenant Dan. H. Alley, Company G, Third Texas Cavalry, will prove of interest:

"I was in command of General W. H. Jackson's scouts, and, in 1864, with five men, was on a reconnoitering expedition in Bolivar county, Mississippi. One evening we had struck camp—that is to say, we had scattered out among the houses of the immediate neighborhood, two or three in a place, so as not to crowd or impose upon the citizens. Walter Boster and another man, whom I do not now recall, but think he was John Nelson, went to a house about a mile distant, and, in a very short time, Boster came back to me, and reported that he thought Dr. Peters was at the house where he was stopping, but was not sure. I instructed him to return, and keep out a strict watch during the night, and ascertain, if possible, if the suspected person was Peters; and that if he ascertained, beyond doubt, that it was Peters, to arrest and hold him. After supper, the ladies of the family and Dr. Peters were engaged in a game of cards. The lady of the house was a niece of Peters. Accidentally, one of them called his name, so as to leave no doubt, on the mind of Boster, as to his identity. Shortly after this he laid off his pistols, a pair of Smith & Wesson, with one of which he killed the General. Boster now arrested him. He made no resistance—probably because they 'had the drop on him.' He appeared very much incensed at such a procedure, and forthwith dispatched a negro messenger for me, desiring that I 'come over' and explain. I sent Boster instructions to guard him until morning, when I would come over 'and explain.' I went over early the next morning. He demanded my authority for causing his arrest, etc. I informed him that I was a Confederate officer, and that I arrested him for the killing of Major-General Earl Van Dorn, and that there was a standing order for his arrest. He desired to know what disposition I would make of him. I informed him that I reported to Brigadier-General W. H. Jackson, and that he was destined to that officer's head-quarters. He stated that he knew I was a Texan, and that I intended to kill him, as he had learned that the Texas Brigade had vowed vengeance against him. I assured him that he should be protected so long as he conducted himself docilely. He slept none, but was engaged in writing the greater part of the night. I presumed he was writing his will, as he evidently believed we would kill him. On our way to head-quarters, he talked freely about the affair; abused his wife, and General Van Dorn, but was more bitter against Mrs. Peters than the General. He said that he had parted with her once before for a similar offense, committed in connection with a man other than General Van Dorn. He stated that he only condoned her fall from virtue on account of his children. He told me that he had caught Van Dorn at his house two nights before the killing; that Van Dorn ran out of, and under the house; that he pursued, and dragged him forth by the hair of the head. Van Dorn was intoxicated at the time, and begged for his life, which he spared on condition that he would visit his house no more, and that he would sign writings to that effect; and also admit, in writing, that he (Van Dorn) had been too intimate with his wife. On the morning of the murder, he stated that he visited the office of Van Dorn to have him comply with these promises, and that Van Dorn exclaimed: 'Take the door, you ——— puppy!' whereupon, he drew his pistol and fired. I took him to General Jackson's head-quarters, which were situated about fifteen miles from Canton, Mississippi. Efforts were made to take him from me by writ of *habeas corpus*, but I informed them that I would oppose any such attempt with force, and that, if they forced me to extremities, I would kill him myself, in preference to surrendering him. General Jackson had him conveyed to Meridian, where the court was in session for the trial of all military causes. I learned, subsequently, that he was tried and acquitted, and that he returned home, and took to his bosom the twice-discarded wife. Of this latter statement, however, I can not vouch, as it is merely hearsay. As well as I can remember, the scouts with me at the time were: Walter Boster—killed near Atlanta, Georgia, in a personal difficulty, (he was as brave a man as ever lived)—Edgar Dade, J. W. Grimes, and John Nelson; the former were Texans, the latter, a Mississippian. Very much of his conversation in regard to Mrs. Peters and Van Dorn was unsuitable for print, and I have, consequently, omitted the greater portion of it."

The funeral of the dead General was very impressive and solemn. The command was mounted, and drawn up on either side of the street. The body, in a metallic casket, was laid in the hearse; on the head of the coffin reposed his Mexican *sombrero*, bearing a gold Texas star; along the breast reposed his gold-hilted sword, a present from the State of Mississippi; at the foot of the coffin, stood his military boots. Following the hearse was his horse, bridled and saddled. As the hearse passed down the lines, the officers and men saluted their dead chieftain with the saber; and, though extremest silence reigned, many an eye was moist. Especially did his escort seem to realize their loss. They were men of the old army, who had followed the fortunes of the dashing "Major" into the Confederate army, and had come to look upon the General as little children do a father. We repeat, that the death of General Van Dorn was a great calamity to the Confederacy. Upon the death of the General, the cavalry corps was broken up; General Forrest, with his division, remaining in Tennessee, and the brigades of Whitfield (Texas), Cosby, and Ferguson, were organized into a division, over which was placed Brigadier-General W. H. Jackson, a cultured gentleman, and a brave, efficient officer, and a native of the State of Tennessee.

Grant had now inaugurated his titanic operations against the heroic city of Vicksburg, and Jackson's Division was ordered to the scene of operations. Probably a month was consumed in the arduous march, which afforded no incident worthy of note. Several days before we arrived in the vicinity of the doomed city, the terrible artillery duel, that was progressing day and night, could be distinctly heard. The city being closely invested, there remained but little for the cavalry to do but cover the front of the relieving army being organized by General Joseph E. Johnston. Preparations were finally made for crossing the Big Black river—and Breckinridge's Division, with the pontoon-train, were actually on the bank of the river—when intelligence came of the surrender. Immediately, the Confederate infantry fell back to Jackson, and the cavalry was left to dispute the advance of General Sherman, who marched on Jackson at the head of near 30,000 men. During these operations, the Texas Brigade was commanded by General J. W. Whitfield—Colonel Ross being in temporary command of another brigade, and operating in the Tennessee valley.

During the three days of Sherman's march from Vicksburg to Jackson, the command was under fire incessantly, and often and again did the impetuosity of their attacks force Sherman to deploy a division to clear the audacious troopers from his front. The "siege of Jackson," so-called, the retiring of Johnston to Brandon, and, eventually, the departure of Sherman for Vicksburg, are all too well-known to require repetition here. *Vide* conclusion of this chapter for additional details.

During the remainder of the summer and autumn, the Texas Brigade remained in front of Vicksburg, having an occasional skirmish to break the dull monotony of camp-life.

About this time—in the fall of 1863—General Whitfield, whose health was feeble, sought service in the Trans-Mississippi Department, and Colonel L. S. Ross, of the Sixth Texas Cavalry, was named Brigadier-General, and assigned to the command of the Texas Brigade. So identified did the General become with his brigade, that ever afterward it was known as Ross' Brigade. General Ross was quite young when the "wreath and stars" were conferred upon him, but he had been inured to war from his youth up. His father, Captain S. P. Ross, was, in the early days of Texas, a compatriot of Ben McCulloch, Hayes, Chevallie, and did good service on the exposed frontier against savage Indian and marauding Mexican. Under the brave father's lead, the no less gallant son took his first lessons in war, and the truthful incidents connected with the youth of General Ross, if presented in print, would appear as a romance. The strong individuality of General Ross marked him from the commencement of the civil war, while his magnetic nature, and noble qualities of head and heart, made him almost the idol of the whole brigade. The boys were proud of their dashing young General, and I doubt if he would have accepted a Major-General's commission, unless conditioned that the old brigade should remain with him. As one instance, among hundreds that could be given, I copy from a recent letter from B. P. Simmons, who was a gallant soldier of the Sixth Texas Regiment of Cavalry, showing the affection that existed between the General and the men:

"I was with the command at the battle of Corinth, where I was wounded; and, right here, I wish to make mention of General Ross (God bless him!), who assisted me in getting off the field of battle. I had the calf of my leg shot away in a charge we made on Friday evening, when I was conveyed back to the hospital—I suppose some three miles to the rear—and was placed on a blanket between Goodson King and Spearman, both belonging to Company D, Sixth Texas. Both of them had their legs shattered by grape-shot. King died that night, and Spearman the next morning, about eight o'clock. As the army retreated on Saturday morning, General Ross placed me on his own horse, and carried me safely out of danger."

This is an incident that we read of in the exploits of ideal heroes in romances; but how seldom do we ever come upon the incident verified, as in this instance?

General Ross was fortunate in the selection of his staff officers. Captain D. R. Gurley, than whom a more perfect and accomplished gentleman does not exist, was the Assistant Adjutant-General, and served his chief, throughout the war, with intelligence, fidelity, and signal courage. Next to the General, I doubt if Captain Gurley was not the most popular man in the brigade.

In January, 1863, the brigade was sent to guard a train, loaded with arms for the army, in the Trans-Mississippi Department. The weather was bitter cold, the smaller streams being frozen over. The men were thinly clad, and suffered terribly. The roads in the swamp being found impassable by wagons, the rifles were taken from the boxes, and each man, from the General down, took two guns and carried them to the river, where, with much difficulty, they were crossed over—an artillery duel, between a gun-boat and the Confederate battery, being in progress all the while. Sherman was now preparing for his celebrated raid through Mississippi, and General Ross hastened to the theater of operations. An expedition of gun-boats and transports, started up the Yazoo river about the same time that Sherman set out. To this latter expedition, General Ross paid his attention. The enemy landed at Satartia, and attacked Ross' Brigade, which was drawn up in line of battle just out the village. The Texans repulsed the enemy, who were mostly negroes, with white officers, and closely pursued them to the water's edge, when Ross retired from the guns of the boats. The action was sharp, hot, and decisive. General Ross was at the head of his column, encouraging his men by word and example. The repulsed enemy steamed up the river. At Liverpool, General Ross attacked the enemy in his floating fort. The Texan sharpshooters soon caused the port-holes to be closed, and the enemy turned, and retreated down the river. Had not General Ross been called to the assistance of General Polk, who commanded the Confederate army in front of Sherman, it is not at all problematical that he would have driven the enemy down the Yazoo, and forced him to seek refuge behind the walls of Vicksburg.  A double-quick march now commenced for General Polk.  General Ross fell in Sherman's rear, and, by many annoying and persistent attacks, materially retarded that General's march.

At Marion, Ross engaged the greater portion of the Union army all day in skirmishes, as if intending to attack in force.  Here Sherman, doubtless, intended awaiting the arrival of General Smith, who, with 15,000 men, was *en route* from Memphis join him, intending, perhaps, when thus re-enforced, to march against and capture Mobile.  Smith was advancing down the Mobile & Ohio Railroad, confronted by the indomitable Forrest.  Ross was ordered to proceed, with the utmost dispatch, to General Forrest's assistance.  Off the Texans started; but, on the second day, intelligence reached Ross that Forrest had routed his enemy, and that the demoralized army of Smith was flying in confusion toward Memphis.  This startling intelligence was sufficient to cause General Sherman to retrace his steps, also.  General Ross was now ordered to the Yazoo, to complete the job he had just commenced when ordered away—*i. e.*, clear the river and valley of the enemy.  The column took up the line of march for Bentonville—distant from Yazoo city about ten miles, and being connected with it by a plank-road.  The brigade passed through the village, and were encamping—two regiments, in fact, had gone into camp, and the battery was planted facing down the Yazoo road—when, like a clattering apparition, two of the Texan scouts dashed into camp hotly pursued by about two hundred negro cavalry.  The battery gave them a startling salute that emptied several saddles, when General Ross mounted his horse, and shouting: "Charge them!" went clattering down the road, followed by his men, in enthusiastic confusion.  The "black apes," as the boys called the negro soldiers, were pursued into the lines of Yazoo city, and the weary and victorious Texans camped

---

NOTE.—During the operations on the Yazoo, two young men of the Sixth Texas were brutally murdered by the enemy, after surrender; and thus was inaugurated an informal "war to the knife," which claimed many victims who otherwise would only have experienced the rigors of captivity.

about a mile in front of their lines. Finally, after one or two days spent in skirmishing, General Ross determined to attack them. A detachment of ten men from Company A, Third Texas, drove in the pickets, which movement was followed up by the advance of the whole brigade. The enemy was driven into their bomb proofs, which were so effectually sealed by the Texan sharpshooters, that not a Federal gun could be heard. The Texans charged into the city, and drove the enemy aboard of the gun-boats, and these iron monsters found it convenient to ride at anchor in the middle of the river. The guns of the boats were practically useless at such short range, as the river being higher than the country immediately around, the shells passed harmlessly over the heads of the Texans into the hills.

Night closed the scene, and General Ross drew off his men to the camp of the previous evening, intending to pay his respects to the enemy again in the morning. But the commander of the "black apes" did not wish another repetition of the "sealing-up process," consequently, he discreetly slipped aboard his boats, weighed anchor, and steamed for Vicksburg, to compare notes of failure and disappointment with General Sherman. The remainder of the campaign was confined to repelling raids from Vicksburg until about the last of April, when General Ross was ordered to re-enforce the army of General Johnston in North Georgia. This long march was prosecuted in a somewhat leisurely manner, the command often halting, for several days, to recuperate. One of these halting-places was Tuscaloosa, Alabama, at which point two members of Company A, Third Texas— Harvey Gregg and —— Gray—were drowned in the Black Warrior river.

Ross' Brigade reached the army of General Johnston as it was crossing the Etowah river, and was immediately assigned to duty at the front. From this time on, to the fall of Atlanta, the brigade was daily under fire. For two months the men did not change their apparel, partook of only cold rations, and, during most of the time, were exposed to heavy rains—both from the clouds, and from the throats of the enemy's guns. The engagement at New Hope Church was a brilliant action, and reflected luster on Texan arms. General Ross brought on the engagement, and the brigade, with those of Granberry and Ector, repulsed, with heavy loss, a greatly superior corps of the enemy. General Johnston warmly congratulated the troops engaged, upon the immediate field of battle.

The lines of Sherman were now fast closing around Atlanta, yet the wily old chief of the Confederates disputed, stubbornly, each inch of ground, and every advance of the Northern army was dearly paid for. Sherman became impatient, or doubted the eventual success of his movements in front, and had recourse to cavalry raids in the rear of the Confederate position, with a view to cutting their lines of communication. General McCook, with an expeditionary force of cavalry numbering about 5,000, passed the left flank of the Confederate position, and gained the rear; but so closely was he pursued by the Texas Brigade and the Eighth Texas Cavalry (the Terry Rangers), that but little opportunity was allowed him to destroy the railroad. Finally, he was brought to bay near Jonesboro, and attacked so vigorously, that his forces were demoralized, many were captured, and the remainder put to flight.* Not being fully satisfied with the result of McCook's failure, General Sherman dispatched General Kilpatrick on a similar mission.

The Legion was on picket. This brave old regiment, handled by its gallant Colonel, John H. Broocks, contested the ground to the last, but was compelled to yield to overwhelming numbers, and Kilpatrick turned the flank of the Confederate position, and proceeded to the rear; but the vigilant Ross soon had his men in the saddle and in pursuit. A little after daylight, Ross struck the enemy in the flank, and inflicted considerable loss on him. But the innumerable attacks made on this raiding column by Ross' Brigade, are now impossible of description. Suffice it to say, that no opportunity for attack was allowed to go unimproved. Finally, Kilpatrick attempted to enter Lovejoy Station, and finding a division of infantry there, retired. General Ross had formed his brigade in the enemy's rear, expecting to be supported by the brigades of Cosby and Ferguson—neither of which put in an appearance. Finding the infantry too strong for him, and meeting with an unexpected attack from Ross in the rear, Kilpatrick attempted to intimidate the Texans by a furious shelling, and then charged

---

* In this engagement fell William L. Thornton, the pride of his regiment and friends. Texas never possessed a son who gave greater promise than he. Daring and brave to a fault, he was sensitive, and refused promotion frequently tendered.

through the line—a feat by no means remarkable, when we consider that Ross did not have exceeding five hundred men, and Kilpatrick as many thousands. Add to this the fact that the Texans were dismounted, and armed with short guns—not having a bayonet in the brigade—and it will not be wondered at that they did not repulse a cavalry charge of ten times their number. Ross lost two or three men killed and wounded, and about thirty prisoners, many of whom escaped the first night.

Scarcely had the charging column passed the line, when the indomitable Ross had his bugler to sound the rally, and, in an incredibly short space, renewed his unceasing attacks upon the enemy's rear. From this time on, Kilpatrick found no rest, and, evidently, was bent upon the sole plan of making the best of his way out of a bad scrape. He was somewhat more fortunate than his predecessor, McCook, and made Sherman's lines in pretty good order. As the author was captured in the charge at Lovejoy Station, the remainder of the narrative is told as it was told to him. Nothing like a minute description has been attempted in the hasty tracing of the Georgia campaign. Each day was a battle, without characteristics to distinguish it from the battle of the day before, or that of the next day; and that campaign, being, as it was, one series of contests, will always defy the efforts of the conscientious historian. He may deal with it in the concrete—in the abstract, never.

## ADDENDA IN REGARD TO THE SIEGE OF VICKSBURG, AND OTHER OPERATIONS OF THE YEAR 1863.

The Texas Brigade, in command of General J. W. Whitfield, took up the line of march from Maury county, Tennessee, for the purpose of re-enforcing the army of General Johnston, who was attempting the deliverance of Pemberton's beleaguered legions in Vicksburg, on May 19, 1863. On arriving in Mississippi, Colonel L. S. Ross was placed in command of a brigade composed of his own regiment, the Sixth Texas Cavalry, and Colonel Pinson's regiment—the First Mississippi Cavalry—and dispatched on an expedition in the Tennessee valley. The remainder of the Texas Brigade commenced duty on the line of the Big Black, which service consisted of frequent skirmishes with the enemy on the other bank, picket duty, scouting expeditions, etc.

LIEUTENANT-COLONEL JOHN H. BROOCKS.

The head-quarters of General Whitfield were established at Bolton's Depot.

The vigilant and courageous Colonel Broocks, and his veteran Legion, signalized themselves upon this field by valuable and conspicuous services rendered on more than one occasion; among which, we are enabled to record the following: One day the Federals were grazing some one hundred and fifty beeves in threatening proximity to the line of demarcation—the river. Colonel Broocks, upon his own motion, silently crossed the river, and, by a rapid movement, dispersed the guard and captured the cattle; all of which he delivered to the Commissary of the brigade, much to the gratification of his not overfed comrades of the other regiments.

On July 5, the Legion went on picket duty in its turn. On the 6th, General Sherman commenced advancing eastward, and 16,000 of his men crossed at Messenger's Ferry. The Legion was posted, in a slightly-elevated wood, on the east side of the river, and commanded an open field through which the enemy must pass. The position was one eminently adapted to a stubborn defense, and the gallant Broocks improved its natural advantages by a determination truly heroic, to hold his ground until re-enforcements should come to his aid, or he be driven from the field by the mere momentum of overwhelming odds. For four hours did the Legion hold the position against all efforts of the enemy to dislodge them; and it was only after the Federals had gained a foothold on the eminence, and, despairing of assistance, that the iron-willed officer consented to lead his men from the field rendered glorious by their valor; a movement which the brave Texans executed with perfect order. The report of prisoners taken on the field, represented the Federal loss as very heavy, and rumor stated that General Osterhaus was wounded, or killed. The primary cause of the stubborn resistance of the Legion, was the appearance of an impostor, who represented himself to Colonel Broocks as a Confederate officer, and showed a dispatch purporting to come from General Johnston, in which the commander doubted the fall of Vicksburg, and urged Colonel Broocks to dispute the advance of the enemy until he could ascertain the strength of the force in his front. The Legion leisurely fell back to the line of the Ninth Texas Cavalry, about two miles distant, which regiment had come forward to relieve the Legion. Although his men and horses sadly needed rest, food, and sleep, Colonel Broocks complied with the urgent request of Colonel Jones, of the Ninth, to form the Legion in supporting distance of his regiment. The enemy soon began the advance, and opened upon the Ninth with artillery and deafening volleys of small arms. Colonel Broocks hastened to the assistance of his brave young comrade, Colonel Jones, and continued to dispute the ground with the enemy, foot by foot, from position to position, until ten o'clock at night, when the storm of battle lulled. The contestants slept upon the field, in the midst of their respective killed and wounded, separated by but a few hundred yards. General Whitfield, with the Third Regiment, came up in the night, and, with the early dawn of the morning, the contest was renewed with redoubled exertions on either side. On every foot of ground, from Bolton's Depot to Clinton, a distance of eight miles, did the brave old Whitfield, and his indomitable veterans, struggle with the overwhelming numbers of Sherman, and force them to pay dearly for every advantage gained.

At Clinton, the brigade remained two or three days, as the enemy did not advance. At the end of this time, and when one-half of the brigade was absent from camp in quest of forage for the horses, excepting the Legion, the Federals resumed the offensive. General Whitfield dispatched Colonel Broocks immediately to the support of the skirmishers, and soon the Legion, formed in an open field upon a slight elevation, the cynosure of hundreds of admiring eyes, was engaged with the enemy. With such coolness, tact, and decision, did the gallant Broocks handle his men on this occasion, that he elicited the thanks of his superiors in command, and won for himself, and his incomparable Legion, the admiration of all. A young Mississippian, who was in the lines of the enemy, and present in the field-hospitals the night of the engagement, subsequently reported the killed and wounded of the enemy as approximating near one hundred. The loss of the Legion was slight.

Late in October, 1863, the Legion, commanded by its brave and efficient Colonel, E. R. Hawkins, together with Company E, of the Third (Lieutenants Soap and B. T. Roberts), were ordered to report to Colonel L. S. Ross, commanding the temporary brigade before mentioned, to which had been added Willis' Battalion of Texas Cavalry. It had been the original purpose of the expedition for Ross to re-enforce General Forrest, and, together, attempt the capture of Memphis. But, at Grenada, Ross learned that General Forrest was otherwise engaged, and had, consequently, abandoned his purpose in regard to the original conception. Colonel Ross was summoned, with his command, to Pontotoc, Mississippi, by General S. D. Lee; and his brigade, together with that of General Ferguson, and some companies of artillery, were organized into a division. The command was reviewed at Pontotoc by General Joseph E. Johnston, and there witnessed the hanging of a Federal spy, who was dressed in Confederate uniform, and who, probably, was a member of the Fourth Illinois Infantry.

From Pontotoc, the division moved into North Alabama, where General W. T. Sherman, at the head of some 30,000 men, was marching along the railroad, up the Tennessee river, *en route* to re-enforce the beaten army of Rosecranz, at Chattanooga. General Lee proceeded to dispute the passage of the valley with the enemy, and so skillfully did he employ the limited means at his disposal, that General Sherman found it impossible to make the celerity of movement necessary to arrive at Chattanooga in time to succor his comrades there. The fighting was incessant, and the weather bitter cold, which called upon the thinly-clad men for the exercise of all the fortitude and endurance that they could summon.

Colonel John H. Broocks, with nine companies detailed from the Sixth Texas, Legion, and First Mississippi, was dispatched to destroy the railroad from Bear creek, eastward. This was an arduous and fatiguing task, but the men performed it faithfully—burning the ties, heating the rails, and bending them double. While in the performance of this duty, Colonel Broocks was apprised of the fact that General Lee had fallen back on Bear creek, and was preparing to give battle. Broocks promptly repaired to the scene at the head of his nine companies, and participated in the spirited engagement which ensued. But it was in vain that General Lee attempted, with his small force, to check the progress of Sherman's legions. He was driven from the field by the mere weight of numerical superiority. General Sherman crossed the Tennessee thirty-five miles below Tuscumbia, and thus avoiding the lion in his way, proceeded to his destination.

Colonel Ross now set out for Mississippi with his command, and, at Okolona, the Legion left for the brigade proper, which was now commanded by Colonel H. P. Mabry, of the Third—General Whitfield having, in consequence of continued ill-health, gone home. The Legion reported to Colonel Mabry at a point about twenty miles west of the town of Canton. General Ross, with the remainder of the brigade—Sixth Texas, First Mississippi, and Willis' Battalion—moved northward from Okolona to intercept a body of Federal cavalry who were raiding in that section. Ross met the body in battle, defeated it, and drove it into Memphis, when he returned to Canton, and assumed command of the Texas Brigade; Colonel H. P. Mabry, at the same time, being assigned to the command of a brigade in the cavalry corps of Lieutenant-General N. B. Forrest. From this period, until the termination of the war, it is believed Colonel Mabry remained with the cavalry corps of General Forrest; commanding, at first, a brigade, and, subsequently, a division. The author regrets, exceedingly, that he has no data upon which to predicate a narrative of the sterling services of the gallant Mabry while attached to this command. But to have won the confidence and esteem of the incomparable Forrest to such a degree that he would not consent to part with his Texan Lieutenant, should have sufficed for the ambition of any man. Of Colonel H. P. Mabry, it can be truthfully said that he possessed all the higher qualities that enter into the heroic composition; and, through his accomplishments as a ripe scholar and profound jurist, he is no less conspicuous in the walks of civil life than he was on the field. Colonel Mabry has a future that will yet shed a luster on the annals of Texas.

In the progress of the fight with McCook, Lieutenant T. J. Towles, of Company G, Third Texas Cavalry, was dangerously wounded, and remained, for some time, within the lines of the enemy. Says Lieutenant Towles:

"As I was sitting, with my back to a tree for support, my clothing saturated with blood, from the loss of which I was very faint and weak, General McCook, accompanied by some members of his staff, halted in front of me, and the General remarked: 'Major, you appear to be suffering.' I replied that I thought I was mortally wounded, and requested surgical aid. The General replied that he could not even give his own wounded the necessary attention, and said, apologetically: 'You have been a soldier long enough to know how these things are, and you must not think hard of me.' He wished to know what forces were opposing him on the immediate field. I replied that he could form as correct an estimate of their numerical strength as I could, as the divisions of Jackson, Wheeler, and Roddy were present; whereupon, he remarked to his staff: '*We must get out of this!*' and immediately rode away."

This revelation of Lieutenant Towles explains the panic with which McCook's men were seized, when General Ross, soon after, bore down upon them in the headlong charge which routed and dispersed them. Too much praise can not be accorded this brave officer for his fortitude and loyal devotion to his country's cause, though suffering from excruciating pains that amounted to agony. Captain Towles is now a prosperous merchant of Camden, Van Zandt county, Texas, and is worthy the homage of all who love the true, the noble, and the brave. Long may his voyage of life be fanned by the breezes of prosperity, is the wish of his friend, the author. Lieutenant T. J. Towles was long the brave, vigilant, and efficient commander of the brigade scouts, and as such, was the eyes and ears of the command. In the discharge of this hazardous service, he won the confidence of his commanding general, and we always slept with a sense of security when the faithful Towles was on duty. Lieutenant Dan. H. Alley performed a similar duty for the division commander, General W. H. Jackson, and was always equal to any emergency that might arise. Of him we have spoken elsewhere.

During the Mississippi campaign, the chivalrous Lieutenant Hill Taylor commanded the brigade scouts, and during the intervals between his engagements with the enemy, found time to cement one upon the basis of love with a *faire ladie* of Silver creek, whom he led to the hymeneal altar when the "cruel war was over."

Distinguished as solitary scouts, or spies, the names of B. S. Triplett, and J. W. Montgomery — the present efficient Sheriff of Rains county — were pre-eminent. Triplett fell at the hands of an assassin, as elsewhere stated, but Wiley Montgomery is winning as many encomiums in the civic walks of life, as he did in the more hazardous paths of war. He is worthy of all the honors his fellow-citizens may confer upon him.

# CHAPTER IX.

### THE BEGINNING OF THE END.

During these latter days, when the fate of the Confederacy was trembling in the balance, and Titans grappled for the possession of the "Gate City," the scene shifts so frequently that the *camera* fails to retain an impression. The visit of President Davis; the removal of General Johnston; the placing of General Hood in command of the army, are events yet remembered. Then came Sherman's erratic move to the rear, which sealed the fate of Atlanta. In all these rapid movements Ross' Brigade bore its banner with honor, and signalized its prowess on twenty of the bloodiest fields of the tragic drama.

It was theirs to lead the Confederate advance; theirs to participate, as infantry, in the stubborn fight, and theirs, finally, to cover the gloomy retreat. While the infantry were enjoying short respites of repose in camp, from their arduous duties in the field, Ross' men formed a cordon of safety between them and the enemy—where sleepless vigilance was the price of security. No historian will ever recount the many acts of individual heroism performed in the wild mountain passes of North Georgia by the Texas scout; no record will ever keep for admiring posterity the midnight attack and repulse. The future will but know the general legend, that Ross and his braves were tried by ordeals that taxed to their utmost the highest qualities of our nature, and that they came forth from the fiery saturnalia of demoniac war as gold purified from the crucible. True to every trust, their sublime devotion wavered not, nor did their heroic exertions relax even when the hand of Fate had written the Confederacy's epitaph above the hopes of its people, and craven manhood deserted the colors of their allegiance, and sought ignoble security behind the devastating lines of the enemy. The last rally of the bugle found them as ready to mount as did the first, when cheered by the smiles of wives and sweethearts in far distant Texas.

It is not our province to follow the rapid moves of the columns on this gigantic field of war. Sherman commenced his "march to the sea," and Hood set out for Nashville. General Ross was ordered with his brigade to take the advance, and to proceed to the vicinity of Decatur and Tuscumbia, Ala. This march was performed quietly enough, as no enemy at all was encountered. At Decatur, General Ross awaited the arrival of General Hood, who, with the main army, arrived in a few days, and went into camp, remaining there nearly a week, to allow rest and refreshment to the tired men. During the halt, however, activity reigned in the commissary and ordnance departments; and the necessary ammunition and provisions were gotten ready for the purposed campaign. Again, Ross was ordered to take the advance. The Tennessee river was crossed, and the column headed for Nashville. At the Tennessee river the enemy's cavalry was encountered; but, after several spirited engagements, General Ross drove them from his front. The march was necessarily slow and tedious. The cavalry of the enemy was re-enforced by overwhelming numbers, and, no sooner had Ross driven a body from his front, than he was attacked by a fresh contingent, which arduous service told heavily on men and horses. Even the night brought but little relief, for both General and men were in arms during the entire night. Thus Ross led the advance into Tennessee, literally cutting a pathway through the multitudinous enemy for the march of Hood's army. A few miles south of Pulaski, Tenn., a large force was descried drawn up in line of battle, and occupying a very advantageous position. Ross did not hesitate a moment, but commenced preparations to attack, though it was evident that they out-numbered the Texans in the ratio of ten to one.' The Legion was deployed to the left; the Ninth to the right, and the Third and Sixth advanced as the center. All thought a hotly-contested engagement was imminent. But, after some heavy skirmishing, the enemy, evidently thinking discretion the better part of valor, left the field precipitately, and fell back on Pulaski. At this place, General Ross discovered the enemy posted in force, and so dispatched General Hood, in the meantime, however, annoying the Federals with his skirmishers and sharpshooters. Hood came up with the army, and directed Ross to turn the left flank of the enemy, and gain his rear. Seeing Ross in the execution of this movement, the enemy abandoned his position, and once more retired in the direction of Nashville, to which point all the clouds of war seemed now converging for the coming storm. Ross pursued the retreating Federals; and, from Pulaski to Columbia, scarce a moment passed that the eager Texans were not on their heels. In this pursuit many prisoners were taken, and some wagons. At Columbia it was understood that the enemy would give battle. Cheatham's Division had been sent lower down the river to cross, so as to gain the enemy's rear. Arriving in front of Columbia, General Hood directed General Ross to cross Duck river some miles above the city, and gain the enemy's rear—a move he executed with neatness and dispatch, taking position on the pike between Spring Hill and Franklin. General Ross at once dismounted his men, and attacked the enemy in his front (Federal rear) with vigor. Simultaneously with the report of Ross' guns, General S. D. Lee attacked the enemy in Columbia. It evidently was Hood's design that Cheatham should have re-enforced Ross' Brigade with his division of infantry, and capture the army of Schofield at Columbia. Lee drove the enemy into town; and Schofield bent his energies now to drive Ross from his rear—now become his front—that he could retire. All that day the unequal contest raged. The brave young hero was dismounted and at the head of his columns; and his clear, ringing voice was often heard above the din of conflict, encouraging his men to maintain the unequal grapple. Anxiously, but in vain, did Ross look for Cheatham. He felt that his skeleton brigade could not much longer stand up before the terrible odds pitted against it. The long hours seemed interminable in their weary course; and the guns of the enemy thundered their vomitings of iron hail into the decimated ranks of the Texans. The field of battle was the narrow turnpike, and the vast numbers of the enemy did not avail as they would on the open field. To the deafening volleys of the enemy's fifty guns, the unerring rifles of the Texans defiantly replied. In vain did the Federal infantry charge the position time after time, as if to sweep, by mere weight of numbers and momentum, the audacious Texans from their path. But Ross, sword in hand, his face blackened with the smoke of battle, met them each time with a counter-charge, to retire, when the spasmodic death-grapple was over, sullenly to his old position. Ross appeared as personating the character of Leonidas in the pass of a western Thermopylæ. Finally, the sun set as if ashamed to witness the scene of slaughter. As the thunders of battle lulled temporarily, the groans of the wounded—piled on the narrow pike indiscriminately with the dead—were heard, often begging in piteous accents for water. Ross learned from a citizen that General Cheatham was not more than a mile distant. Assuredly, then, the long and anxiously-expected re-enforcement will soon arrive. This hope imparts to the indomitable young chieftain new resolution, and nerves his heart with determination to hold the pass at all hazards. He communicates the high and unselfish resolve to his men, and is answered by cheers of enthusiasm. They feel that they hold in their hands the key of the position; and that the muse of history is contemplating their acts. They appreciate the magnitude of the trust reposed in them, and swear to be faithful at the price of life itself.

Doubtless, General Hood imagined that it was the legions of Cheatham that were staying the progress of Schofield's divisions, and felt that victory was in his grasp. And, if Cheatham had come, how different would have been the result. Hood did all that it was in the power of mortal man to do. His orders were disobeyed, and Napoleon himself would have failed, under similar circumstances. But the lull in the storm of battle was only temporary. Again the enemy, with re-enforcements drawn from the front of Lee, where the combatants had ceased for the night, renewed the contest with redoubled efforts. He was struggling for existence, and desperation characterized his attempts to extricate himself from the enveloping lines of the determined Confederates. The darkness of the night was lit up by the lurid glare of a hundred cannon, and their thunders reverberating among the rocks and hills, sounded as if pandemonium had settled upon the earth. Volley after volley of musketry rattled along the lines; the groans of the wounded; the piles of the dead; the shrieks of the combatants, formed a picture in the stygian darkness terrible and sublime! Charge after charge the enemy made on the Texan position; but the indomitable Ross never failed to accept the gage, and always met them on halfway ground. Often the combatants were mixed in inextricable confusion, and friend could not be distinguished from foe. Thus, throughout the entire night did the demoniacal conflict rage; but *Ross held the pike!* With the morning's dawn the enemy ceased firing in front, and concentrated all his available force of infantry, cavalry, and artillery upon the position held by Ross, who, by the mere force of numbers and the utter exhaustion of his men, retired sorrowfully from the pike that had witnessed his unparalleled defense. The Texans retired but a short distance from the field, and sought that repose so much needed, while the army of Schofield was pouring through the gap thus formed, and leading Hood on to the fatal field of Nashville. Had Cheatham re-enforced Ross on the pike, the campaign would have closed at Columbia in a glorious Confederate victory.

Having rested the greater portion of the day, the shades of evening found Ross and his men in the saddle. The enemy was retreating on Franklin; and being stretched along the single pike presented a tempting opportunity to a daring leader to make reprisals—an opportunity that Ross did not neglect. The night was spent by the Texas Brigade in making sudden attacks upon this line; and many prisoners, and wagons containing commissary and quartermaster stores, were captured. The town of Franklin was well fortified, and, doubtless, General Schofield imagined he would be allowed to remain here unmolested—a supposition not justified by the result, for General Hood, immediately upon his arrival, made preparation for an assault. General Ross was dispatched to the right, and up Big Harpeth river, which he crossed. The Texans were here encountered by Brownlow's celebrated "Gray Horse," an excellent body of cavalry. The Ninth Texas was thrown forward as skirmishers; the General holding well in hand the Third, Sixth, and one battalion of the Legion, the remainder of that regiment having been left across the creek as a support. The enemy attacked the Ninth furiously; and, by force of numbers, drove them back. Ross, seeing the condition of affairs, placed himself at the head of his men and charged. The "Gray Horse" met the onset gallantly by a counter-charge, and the two opposing lines absolutely passed through each other; probably an incident without parallel in the whole course of the war.\* Many

---

\*In his desperate encounter with the "White Horse," Colonel Jones, of the Ninth, ran his sword through a Union trooper, and broke it off at the hilt, the blade remaining in the body of his adversary. No one was more conspicuous for daring bravery, in this engagement, than Lieutenant W. J. Cavin, of Company A, Third Texas Cavalry. Sergeant T. J. Cellum, in this engagement, slew in single combat a Union officer, who refused to surrender; himself receiving three pistol-shot wounds in the deadly duel.

hand-to-hand fights ensued; and several of Ross' men were afterward mounted on gray horses captured in the fight. Especially worthy of mention was a personal combat between a Federal non-commissioned officer and J. C. Pritchett, of Company E, Third Texas. Mr. Pritchett killed his man and captured his steed. Again, the "Gray Horse" prepared for another charge. The liberty is taken to quote the language of Lieutenant B. T. Roberts, Company E, Third Texas, to whom the author is indebted for the incidents of the Tennessee campaign: "General Ross told his men to stand firm; that he was there to lead them. He called on the Ninth to rally on him, which was readily done. The enemy, in the meantime, were bearing down on our line furiously; when General Ross, standing straight in his stirrups, shouted 'Forward!' and with drawn saber led the charge in person. At once the opposing lines clashed, and for some time it seemed doubtful which would yield. Ross was ubiquitous, and seemed to bear a charmed life; and was heard to exclaim at the crisis of the engagement, '*Boys, if you don't run, they will!*' And they did. The Texans pursued Brownlow until the fugitives found refuge in night."

While Ross was engaging the "Gray Horse," Hood was storming the ramparts of Franklin. Upon the retreat of the enemy from Franklin, Ross was still kept to the right, and in advance, following the enemy to the very suburbs of Nashville. While General Hood was investing Nashville, General Ross was ordered to cut off re-enforcements to Thomas, expected from Murfreesboro. This he did effectually, capturing stockades and stations between Nashville and Murfreesboro. The result of this brief campaign was three hundred and fifty prisoners, and an immense train loaded with commissary supplies—an invaluable acquisition to General Hood at the time. But General Hood's successes—dearly bought—were at an end. The disastrous battle of Nashville dissipated the hopes of an advance. Indeed, the issue now was the existence of his routed columns. Ross covered the retreat, and hung on the rear of Hood's demoralized army, a barrier to the eagerly-pursuing Federals. This, says Lieutenant Roberts, was the severest service experienced during the war. It being late in December, the weather was intensely cold—freezing all the time—the men were thinly clad, poorly fed, and dejected and disheartened. The Texans were called upon to repulse twenty charges of the enemy's cavalry a day. Nor did night relieve them of their arduous duties; for often they were compelled to stand in line of battle throughout the cold night. But Ross and his men were true to the trust reposed in them, and interposed, as a barrier between the beaten army and its victorious enemy, until the Tennessee river was crossed, which ended the campaign, and virtually, the services of Ross' Texas Brigade. The author would say no more; but point to the record contained in this imperfect narrative of their services.

### ADDENDA.

Through the kindness of Rev. John Hudson, of Hutto, Williamson county, Texas, the author was given access to the diary of his brother, Rev. Edward Hudson, who had been appointed by Colonel Griffith, Chaplain of the Sixth Regiment, Texas Cavalry. Mr. Hudson served some time as a private in Captain "Pete" Ross' company, and bore all the dangers, privations, and hardships, incidental to that position, until promoted Chaplain. In an engagement between Ross' Brigade and the command of General McCook, in July, 1864, near Noonan, Ga., Chaplain Hudson, who accompanied his regiment into the engagement, discovered one of his acquaintances dangerously wounded. He called to a comrade to assist him in removing the wounded man to a place of safety. The two men dismounted, leaving their horses in the care of a third, and immediately proceeded to succor their wounded friend. Having accomplished this humane act, they returned for their horses, but discovered that the enemy had advanced considerably, and that their horses were gone. Chaplain Hudson caught, upon the field, the horse of a Union trooper, mounted him, and proceed in a line diagonally across the field in quest of the missing horses. He was fired upon by a body of the enemy, his horse killed, and himself dangerously wounded. In a recent letter to the author, Rev. John Hudson writes: "At his own request, General Ross had him carried to a private house, and there he remained until the close of the war. Levi Fowler remained with him, and finally brought him home. General Ross (although I never met him) and Levi Fowler occupy a very warm, sacred place in my heart, because of their kind, humane, brotherly treatment of my dear brother. He remained but a short time near Waco; received a suit of clothes and some money from the boys of his old regiment, as a token of their esteem, and went from there to Kemp, Kaufman county, and taught school four years. He resumed preaching soon after settling in Kaufman; but was compelled, in consequence of the result of his wounds, to occupy a sitting posture whenever doing so; and he so continued to preach until his death, which occurred August 17, 1877. He preached a great deal; rode two years as a missionary in the bounds of the "Bacon Presbytery." But he was a great sufferer all the time. His health finally failing, I brought him to my home in Williamson county. He bore his affliction with great fortitude and resignation. His death was one of great peace and triumph; not a dimming veil or cloud obscured his mental horizon."

From Mr. Hudson's diary the following facts in regard to General Ross' campaign in the Tennessee valley, in 1863, are gained; and for which the author is specially thankful, inasmuch as all his efforts to obtain data, upon which to predicate a narrative of this brilliant campaign, have been unavailing. As little else than the dates, and briefest mention of movements, in a general way, are given, the brief story of one of the most successful cavalry expeditions of the war must remain, for the present, at least, but partially told. But to the diary:

"On September 26, 1863, the Sixth Texas Cavalry, and the First Mississippi Cavalry, left Richland, Mississippi, under the command of Colonel L. S. Ross. At Pontotoc, the command was reviewed by General Joseph E. Johnston. Taking up the line of march again, the brigade passed Tupelo, the scene of our infantry encampment the previous summer. From this town, on the Mobile & Ohio Railroad, the brigade proceeded to Tuscumbia, Alabama, on the Tennessee river, where the Fifteenth (Union) Army Corps was stationed. General Ross immediately inaugurated a system of surprises, attacks, etc., that annoyed the enemy intolerably for the space of six days, during which period, night and day, the confused enemy knew not at what moment we would attack him, nor from what point of the compass the attacking party would come. Finally, the Union corps, though numbering nearly ten thousand men, were forced to retire from the Memphis & Charleston Railroad, which it was their duty to hold, and leave it in the possession of their adversary, who could not count over twelve hundred rifles. The enemy was forced to cross the Tennessee river at Eastport, and fall back upon Corinth; thus retarding their purposed re-enforcement of General Rosecranz's army, which was operating against the army of General Bragg in East Tennessee. After considable maneuvering, the brigade made a rapid dash on Moscow, where we had a very spirited fight with the enemy there posted; thence, back, via Holly Springs and Grenada, to Canton, where the remainder of the old brigade were encamped. We here parted with our comrades of the First Mississippi—than which no regiment was composed of more perfect gentlemen or braver soldiers. After this expedition, a feeling of *comraderie* always existed between the Sixth Texas and the First Mississippi. Soon after the arrival of the Sixth Regiment, the brigade moved, in charge of a train of wagons loaded with arms and ammunition for the trans-Mississippi Department. Mention of which is made in its proper place in the narrative.

While the brigade was encamped at Canton, many horses were afflicted with a malady somewhat resembling "blind-staggers," which, in most instances, proved fatal. The general cause assigned, was grazing on a vegetable called "sneeze-weed," of all which the author is ignorant, save only the effects.

Mr. J. Wylie Montgomery, of Company A, Third Texas Cavalry, and at present the efficient sheriff of Rains county, Texas, deserves special mention for his daring bravery in battle, and for his sagacity as a scout, in which peculiarly dangerous service he was long employed, and rendered services of incalculable value to the brigade and division commanders. He is deserving, in all respects, the confidence of his fellow-citizens.

# BIOGRAPHICAL SKETCH

OF

# GENERAL JOHN S. GRIFFITH.

---

In that galaxy of glorious stars, whose effulgence yet lights the memory of the "Lost Cause," though its sun has forever set, none shines with a steadier glow than that consecrated to the name and fame of John S. Griffith. Where palladins seemed to contend in generous emulation for the plaudits of fame, and individual heroism was the daily rule, it would seem invidious to make distinctions. But we can accord all the honors, that are so eminently his due, to this gifted son of Texas, without the disparagement of any one.

Unselfish in his characteristics; brave, though sagacious, as becomes a commander; patriotic in all his impulses; had health been vouchsafed to him, a career of glory and usefulness would have crowned his efforts with success. As it was, by his consummate address on the hardly-contested field of Oakland, and as the central figure of the Holly Springs campaign, he gave ample evidence that he possessed, in a pre-eminent degree, those lofty, necessary qualities that can only fit a man for command in battle. General Griffith was more than a dashing cavalryman, for his analytical mind penetrated far beyond the immediate shock of battle, and took in the salient features of the campaign as a whole. It was he who conceived that master stroke of policy, and was the most efficient agent of its execution—"the Holly Springs Raid." He saved the army of Pemberton, indubitably, by the movement; and, consequently, delayed the fall of Vicksburg many months. On the field of Oakland, he performed for the same army duties, of scarce less vital moment. But we anticipate. John S. Griffith was born in Montgomery county, Maryland, on the 17th day of June, A. D. 1829. His father, Michael B. Griffith, was the son of Captain Henry Griffith, of the Revolutionary army, and a lineal descendant of the historical Llewellen ap Griffith, of Wales. To the influence of his pious mother, who was a daughter of General Jeremiah, and Elizabeth Crabb, a beautiful, cultured, and accomplished lady, whose energy, will, and fortitude were sufficient to surmount the many obstacles and misfortunes that beset her path amid the vicissitudes of life, the subject of this sketch has ever attributed whatever success, under Providence, he has achieved. His parents started in life in affluent circumstances. But forced by some losses in his business (mercantile) Mr. Griffith removed to Jefferson City, Missouri, in the year 1835; and from the latter place to Portland, Missouri, in 1837. Misfortune attended all his efforts to improve the long series of losses, until, when reduced to the paltry capital of one thousand dollars, he removed, April 15th, 1839, to San Augustine county, Texas, with a family of six children, three of whom were girls.

In common with the pioneers of early Texas colonization, theirs was a lot of hardship and privation. Flour cost twenty-five dollars per barrel, and bacon fifty cents per pound. In this situation of affairs, which would have impaired the energies of a man more accustomed to the smiles of success, the father seemed for a space to despond; but the heroine wife and mother rose superior to the occasion, and her high qualities of energy and endurance—and above all, hope eternal, though its realization had been so often deferred, shone with a noon-tide glow that promised to dispel the lowering clouds of adversity that hovered above the devoted heads of her little ones. Such a mother! Is it wonderful that her heroic son should now recall, with moistened eye, her unequal struggle in that frontier home? Her example, though subserving its immediate objects, had a result far more distant and lasting, for it molded in the nature of the boy the admirable qualities that made John S. Griffith a leader of men. How true is the saying of the great Napoleon, that the mother's qualities, good or bad, are always imparted to the son!

This struggle with adversity was accepted without a murmur by young John S., the second son, and, doubtless, he there learned many practical lessons, which had much to do in forming the character of the man.  He received, chiefly at home, the rudiments of an English education; and, in 1850, commenced business as a clerk in a mercantile establishment.  In the following year, he set up on his own account as a merchant, operating wholly on borrowed capital.  Thanks to his industry and economy, the business prospered remarkably; and our young merchant, in December, 1857, was united in marriage to Miss Emily, daughter of John J. and Mrs. Jane Simpson, of Nacogdoches county, Texas.  His business affairs continuing to prosper, he removed, in the year 1859, to Kaufman county, where he engaged in the raising of live stock in connection with his mercantile pursuits.

At the sound of the first tocsin of war, in 1861, Captain John S. Griffith was called to the command of a volunteer company of cavalry raised at Rockwall, Texas.  Captain Griffith tendered the services of his company to Colonel E. Greer, whose regiment, the Third Texas Cavalry, however, was already full.  So ardent were the Rockwall boys, that their liberal Captain offered Colonel Greer to defray their expenses for three months out of his own purse, if allowed to become attached to the regiment for that space.  Why they were not allowed to do so, and as many other companies as desired, must always remain a mystery—seeing that General Price was being driven out of Missouri by an overwhelming Federal force, and that General McCulloch, with a few Arkansas millitia, was awaiting the arrival of the only two regiments coming to his assistance, the Third Texas Cavalry and Third Louisiana Infantry.  Of course, Colonel Greer had no option in the premises, as his authority extended no further than the organization and command of his own regiment.  But it is of interest to discover right here, at the inception of the contest, the commencement of that fatal series of maladministration which contributed more to the wreck of the Confederate cause than the armies of the invader.  The battle of Oak Hills was won through a combination of fortuitous circumstances; and the South relapsed into fancied security.  Had we been beaten there, the result may have aroused the Southern administrations to a sense of the magnitude of the struggle in which they were actors, or hastened the final catastrophe; either of which conclusions was preferable to the protracted, often desultory, and seemingly hopeless manner in which the war was waged on the part of the South.

But Captain Griffith had not long to wait; as soon as Colonel B. Warren Stone commenced the organization of the gallant old Sixth Texas Cavalry, the Rockwall boys were incorporated in this regiment as Company B, and was officered as follows:

John S. Griffith, Captain.

Amos Dye, First Lieutenant.

E. P. Chisholm, Second Lieutenant.

James Truett, Third Lieutenant.

F. M. Nixon, Orderly-Sergeant.

M. B. Cannon, Second Sergeant.

A. C. Richardson, Third Sergeant.

F. Chisum, Fourth Sergeant.

A. W. Hedges, First Corporal.

A. Cummins, Second Corporal.

B. L. Williams, Third Corporal.

John R. Briscoe, Fourth Corporal.

John O. Heath, Ensign.

Allen Anrick, Bugler.

Upon the organization of the regiment, Captain Griffith, who was already a popular favorite with his comrades, was elected Lieutenant-Colonel. The regiment proceeded, as elsewhere stated in these pages, to Arkansas, and reported for duty to General Ben McCulloch. The service here consisted of foraging, scouting expeditions, picket duty, etc.; though the gallant Price and his immortal "Old Guard" were struggling under the "Grizzly Bears" against overwhelming odds. Had the Texans been consulted, they would have sped to the assistance of their struggling Missouri allies. In December, 1861, Colonel McIntosh, in command of a battalion, each from the Third and Sixth Texas Cavalry, the former commanded by Lieutenant-Colonel W. P. Lane, and the latter by Lieutenant-Colonel J. S. Griffith, Whitfield's (Texas) Battalion, and Young's Regiment, Eleventh Texas Cavalry, and a battalion of First Arkansas Cavalry, marched to the relief of General Cooper, who was being driven back by superior forces of hostile Indians. The enemy was encountered on the heights of Chustenahlah, and routed (as elsewhere detailed). The following letter from the gallant and heroic General W. P. Lane will be of interest:

"MARSHALL, TEXAS, February 4, 1881.
"VICTOR M. ROSE, ESQ.:

"*My Dear Sir*—I delayed answering your letter, hoping to find some one more conversant with the incidents of our fight at Chustenahlah than myself; but failing to find any one who would volunteer to do so, I will endeavor to present my recollections of the campaign. On Christmas day, 1861, we moved from camp to attack the Indians, who, we learned, were some ten miles distant. Our force consisted of battalions of Third, Sixth, and Eleventh Texas Cavalry, and Captain Bennett's company, all under command of McIntosh. My battalion being in advance, I detached Captain D. M. Short, with thirty men, to reconnoitre, and to drive back a small party that the enemy had sent out to review us. Finally, Captain Short sent me word that the Indians were posted on the hills in force, and were complacently awaiting our attack. Colonel McIntosh then placed his force in the following order: Sixth Texas, Lieutenant-Colonel Griffith commanding, on the right; Third Texas, Lieutenant-Colonel W. P. Lane commanding, in the center; the Eleventh Texas Cavalry, Colonel Young commanding, together with Bennett's company, on the left. He then ordered me, with the Third, to charge the hill on horseback. The hill was very steep, and just possible for a horse to ascend. I replied, that I would do so with pleasure; and added, 'but if I do not carry the position?' He replied, that, in that event, he would dispatch the Sixth and Eleventh to my aid. I replied, 'All right, but if I do not carry the position I will be at the bottom before the re-enforcements can arrive.' I gave the order for the men to dismount and tighten girths. I then informed the boys that when the command to charge was given, the quicker we got among the Indians the fewer empty saddles we would have. We charged in good style, carrying the hill, and throwing the Indians into confusion. At the same time, Colonel Griffith, on my right, and without orders, led his battalion in a gallant charge, and the Eleventh, and Captain Bennett's company, simultaneously swept around the hill on the left, thus completing the discomfiture of the enemy. Our loss was small; some eight or ten killed, and eighteen or twenty wounded. In my battalion, Lieutenant Durham was mortally wounded, and Major G. W. Chilton slightly. The battle effectually broke up the Indians. We took several hundred prisoners, horses, cattle, sheep, and other property, too numerous to mention.

"Yours, truly, "WALTER P. LANE."

When Colonel McIntosh placed the Sixth in position on the right of the line, his instructions to Colonel Griffith were to *await further orders*. But Colonel Griffith, seeing the intrepid charge of Lane had dislodged the Indians, who were retiring across a deep gulch to the right, very correctly decided that the opportune moment had arrived for striking a decisive blow. Not a moment was to be lost; and, with saber in the left and revolver in the right hand, he led his command in a dashing charge over a seemingly impassable ravine, and spurred his horse up its almost precipitous banks, and was the first of the command to engage in the desperate hand-to-hand encounter that ensued. Emptying his revolver, he borrowed another of one of his captains, and continued the running fight until it was also emptied, when he had recourse to his saber. During the *melee*, Colonel Griffith became separated from his men, and encountered an Indian who was loading his rifle. The Colonel charged upon him, and the Indian recognizing the absence of fear in his opponent, seized his gun as a club. It had been the intention of Griffith to run him through with his saber as he passed him; but now decided to ride him down; and with that purpose reined his horse full upon him, but the Indian agilely stepped aside, and aimed a tremendous blow at his opponent, which knocked the plumed hat of the Colonel to the ground. But simultaneously with the Indian's blow Griffith dealt him a terrible stroke with his saber on the side of the head. Lieutenant Vance opportunely came up and dispatched the Indian.

Griffith now, after a hasty survey of the field, discovered that the enemy were re-forming their lines upon an eminence in front; and that his own men were scattered, every one acting on his own hook. The rally was sounded, and line of battle being formed, when Captain J. W. Throckmorton (since Governor of Texas) rode up to the Colonel and informed him that Lieutenant Gabe Fitzhugh had fallen. Colonel Griffith loved his brave young subaltern, and the announcement of his untimely death brought a tear to his eye. "Comrades!" he exclaimed to the eager men, "Fitzhugh has been killed, and there are his slayers!" About three hundred of the Indians now occupied the rocky eminence in front, and were fully prepared for the threatened attack. "Forward, my brave men!" exclaimed the Colonel, as at their head he dashed up the steep, and among the painted, howling savages, as trusty rifles and repeating pistols were dashing out lives on every side. The men, animated by the ardor of their commander, and by the recklessness of his bearing, fought as if the issue depended upon each individual's exertion. Driven from this position, it was only to retire a short distance and take up another position; and thus four separate charges brought Griffith and his gallant rangers into a hand-to-hand contest with the enemy.

At four o'clock in the afternoon Griffith called in his weary men. They had been engaged incessantly since morning, and were now six miles from the heights of Chustenahlah, where Colonel Lane had so gallantly opened the ball. The enemy had had enough, and were in full retreat. In returning, Colonel Griffith gathered up many wagons, teams, ponies, and other live stock, together with many negroes, women and children, and arrived at camp about night-fall. Colonel Griffith soon reported to Colonel McIntosh to apologize for his disobedience of orders. Said Griffith: "Colonel McIntosh, I felt so well assured that you would have ordered me to do just what I did, had you been present, that I unhesitatingly assumed the responsibility; and since the merit of the move has been tested by its success, I shall in my official report of the engagement state that I moved in conformity to your direction." McIntosh replied that success was vindication; and he further took occasion to compliment the gallantry of Griffith throughout the series of actions. This compliment coming from a man absolutely a stranger to fear, was no idle frame-work of unmeaning words.

In the battle or battles, for it was a series of separate encounters, of Chustenahlah, Colonel Griffith had his horse shot under him, his clothing was perforated by rifle-balls, and a tuft of his whiskers shot away; yet, Saladin-like, as if bearing a talismanic charm, he escaped unhurt, save the blow received with the clubbed rifle, at the hands of the Indian.

At the reorganization of the regiment, near Corinth, in May 1862, Colonel Griffith, against the solicitations of many friends, and, possibly, in violence to the promptings of a commendable ambition, declined to become a candidate for the Colonelcy, and was re-elected to his former position of Lieutenant-Colonel. Colonel Griffith took this decision in consequence of failing health, and the necessity of his visiting home for a brief space; it being understood, at the time, that the Lieutenant-Colonel, or Major, would be detailed to return to Texas on recruiting service.

During General Price's retreat from Abbyville, the Federal General, Washburn, at the head of a considerable force, undertook to intercept the retreat, by marching upon the rear of the Confederate position, and threatened the trains and wounded of Price's corps. Colonel Griffith commanded the Texas Brigade at the time, and attacked Washburn on the field at Oakland, inflicting a heavy loss on him, and driving him from the field—(*vide battle of Oakland*). For the daring gallantry displayed on this occasion, he was the recipient of complimentary letters from Generals Maury, Price, Jackson, and others. The result of the battle at Oakland gave General Price an open road to Grenada, which town he reached in safety, and his weary men were soon seeking the respite from toil, vigilance, and privation, which they so much needed. The campaign was now virtually concluded for the winter; and Colonels Broocks and Griffith often conversed upon the most profitable employment that the cavalry could be assigned to. It was self-evident, that, as matters now stood, they were only consuming the supplies that should be economized for the infantry, which was less able to forage independently. They agreed that the Confederate cavalry, of the Army of the West, should be "massed," and moved into the enemy's lines, where they could repel all smaller bodies, and escape any force too strong to encounter in battle. Thus was the system of heavy cavalry-raiding first advocated. Colonel Griffith adopted this conclusion, and sought to apply it practically to the existing situation of affairs. The Confederate army, beaten in battle, out-numbered by the enemy in the ratio of five to one, poorly clad, poorly fed, pay in arrear, was discontented, not to say demoralized. General U. S. Grant confronted them at the head of a force that was puissant; and the coming spring must inevitably witness another contest against fearful odds, and the army of West Tennessee again defeated, driven into Vicksburg, where its doom would be but a question of time. Colonel Griffith became convinced that of Grant's long line of communication, with his base of supplies at Memphis, the most vulnerable point was Holly Springs, at which place immense quantities of army stores had been collected, and a garrison of about 2,500 men left to guard it. Griffith brooded over this subject, and reviewed it in every conceivable light. A cavalry corps should be organized; the enemy's rear entered, and Holly Springs taken, and all the supplies destroyed; then the railroad should be destroyed as far in the direction of Memphis as possible. Surely this would draw Grant out of Mississippi, and give the Confederate authorities ample time to devise some plan for the defense of the country, and to concentrate sufficient forces with which to execute it. Becoming assured of the feasibility of his project, Colonel Griffith determined to broach the subject to the Commanding General, Lieutenant-General J. C. Pemberton, although he had no acquaintance with him. To this end, he drew up the following letter, which many of the field officers of the brigade also signed at his invitation:

"HEAD-QUARTERS TEXAS BRIGADE,
"CAMP WHARTON, MISS., December 5, 1862.

" LIEUTENANT-GENERAL J. C. PEMBERTON:

"The undersigned, officers of the First Texas Brigade of Cavalry, disclaiming any desire to dictate to the Commanding General my plan, or line of operations he should pursue, would yet beg leave modestly to suggest the propriety of a cavalry expedition into the enemy's rear. We are the more bold to do so, and have less fear of the misconstruction of our motives, when we remember that you have been so recently placed in command over us; and that the multitudinous cares incidental to your responsible position have necessarily, thus far, precluded an examination of the position of the enemy, and as to what is the best employment in which the cavalry, under your command, can be engaged. We, therefore, respectfully submit, if you will fit up a cavalry expedition, comprising three or four thousand men, and give us Major-General Earl Van Dorn, than whom no braver man lives, to command us, we will penetrate the rear of the enemy, capture Holly Springs, Memphis, and other points, and, perhaps, force him to retreat from Coffeeville; if not, we can certainly force more of the enemy to remain in their rear, to protect their supplies, than the cavalry could whip if we remained at the front.

"Very respectfully,

"JOHN S. GRIFFITH,
"Commanding Texas Cavalry Brigade.

"E. R. HAWKINS,
"Commanding First Texas Legion.

"J. H. BROOCKS,
"Major First Texas Legion.

"JILES S. BOGGESS,
"Lieut-Colonel Third Texas Cavalry.

"D. W. JONES,
"Lieut-Colonel Commd'g Ninth Texas Cavalry.

"JACK WHARTON,
"Captain Commanding Sixth Texas Cavalry."

Colonel Griffith forwarded this letter immediately to General Pemberton, and, no one not acquainted with the restless energy of the man, can imagine the night of consuming anxiety and suspense that he passed in awaiting a reply. To his sagacious mind, the memorial suggested the last card left the Confederacy to play with any chance of winning on this board. The Army of West Tennessee must be inevitably crushed whenever Grant should place his legions in motion to execute the fiat of his will. General Pemberton promptly replied the next day, in the following letter:

"HEAD-QUARTERS DEPARTMENT MISSISSIPPI,
"GRENADA, December 6, 1862.

"COLONEL:

"You will furnish me with a report of the events subsequent to the engagement of Oakland. I wish to see you personally, if circumstances will possibly admit of it.

"Very respectfully,

"J. C. PEMBERTON,
Lieutenant-General."

The Commanding General desired a personal interview with the bold ranger who dared to chalk out a campaign to his chief. In the interview which followed, General Pemberton informed Colonel Griffith, that the proposition commended itself to his consideration with much force, and that he would give it careful consideration, etc.

About the 12th, or six days after the interview with General Pemberton, Colonel Griffith received orders to report to General Van Dorn, who was now actively engaged in preparing for the long-desired expedition in rear of the enemy. General Van Dorn's command consisted of the Texas Brigade, Colonel Griffith commanding, 1,500 men; Jackson's Tennessee Brigade, 1,200 men; McCulloch's Missouri Brigade, 800 men. The whole amounting to about 3,500 men. For an account of this famous expedition, the reader is referred to the proper chapter in the body of the narrative.

The services exacted of him, on this expedition, proved so great a demand upon his vital forces that the health of Colonel Griffith, never robust, was seriously impaired; and, in the summer of 1863, he tendered his resignation, and returned to Texas.

The following testimonial from the officers of the "Whitfield Legion," will serve to show, in some degree, the esteem in which Colonel Griffith was held by his comrades:

"CAMP FIRST TEXAS LEGION,

"NEAR SPRING HILL, TENNESSEE, May 10, 1863.

" LIEUTENANT-COLONEL JOHN S. GRIFFITH:

"*Dear Sir*—We, the undersigned, officers of the First Texas Legion, having learned that, in consequence of continued ill-health, you have tendered your resignation, we can not, in justice to our feelings, permit you to quit the service without this testimonial of our appreciation of your services while commanding the brigade, of which our regiment is a part. You were ever the faithful and efficient officer, and, at the same time, the kind and courteous gentleman. Rest assured, sir, that whether you go to some other branch of our country's service, or to your home in the State that we all love so well, you will carry with you the confidence and esteem of the officers and men of the First Texas Legion. With heart-felt wishes for your future welfare, we remain respectfully,

"J. H. BROOCKS,
"Lieut-Colonel Commanding Legion.
"JOHN T. WHITFIELD,
"Major Texas Legion.
"B. H. NORSWORTHY,
"Captain Company E, First Texas Legion.
"C. D. PRESTON,
"Company M, First Texas Legion.
"J. N. ZACHRY,
"Captain Co. A, First Texas Legion.
"J. M. INGRAM,
"Captain Co. C, First Texas Legion.
"B. M. IRWIN,
"First Lieutenant Co. A, Texas Legion.
"W. T. ROGERS,
"Second Lieutenant Co. A, Texas Legion."

Upon his return to Texas, Colonel Griffith was elected a member of the Tenth Legislature; in which body he occupied the responsible position of Chairman of the Committee on Military Affairs. On March 1st, 1864, he was appointed Brigadier-General of State troops, by Governor P. Murrah, and placed in command of District No. 2, which was composed of the counties of Kaufman, Ellis, Navarro, Hill, McLennan, Limestone, Freestone, Leon, Robertson, Falls, Bell, Williamson, Milam, Burleson, Brazos, Madison, Coryell, Bosque; Erath, Hamilton, Comanche, Lampasas, San Saba, Brown, Eastlant, Callahan, Coleman, McCulloch, Mason, Kimble, Menard, Concho, Runnels, Taylor, and Johnston. The duties of the Brigadier-Generals of the State were, "to encourage and form volunteer companies and organizations, of such persons as are not subject to militia or other duty, for local defense, and all necessary police regulations in the counties where such companies may be raised." In his efficient and faithful discharge of the onerous duties encumbent on him in this position, Colonel Griffith elicited the complimentary mention of Governor Murrah, in his message to the Eleventh Legislature. General Griffith continued in command of the "Second District" until the termination of hostilities.

The result of the war left him comparatively poor, he having some twenty-five or thirty slaves; but, with indomitable will, energy, and pluck, upon which his vital forces expend themselves, General Griffith entered the race of life again, and, by dint of industry and good sense, he has accumulated a handsome fortune, and resides in Terrell, Kaufman county, Texas, once more in affluent circumstances.

In 1876, he was elected a member of the Fifteenth Legislature, upon which body devolved the duty of placing in operation the "new constitution." He was appointed Chairman of the Committee on Public Printing, and was successful in defeating the printer in an effort to obtain illegitimate gains at the expense of the State. So assiduous were his labors in this body, that he earned the reputation of being an industrious and untiring legislator. He was, indeed, a "watch-dog" over the public treasury; and lobbyists, shysters, and *chevaliers d'industrie*, shunned him as if his presence was a fatal upas. He was attacked in the newspapers by the printer, who became exasperated at being foiled in his "little game." Griffith responded, and demonstrated the proposed fraud; and, backed by the opinion of the Attorney-General, he had the satisfaction of seeing the "printer" leave the ring demolished in reputation, and all his calculations "*pied*." Several statutes bear the impress of his statesmanship—especially that one making drunkenness in civil officers a misdemeanor. This statute alone is a living monument to his probity of character, and is a work of which he may justly feel proud.

In conclusion, but little remains to be said. General Griffith is yet, comparatively, a young man; and the author, his friend, hopes that he may be spared, by the grim specter of the glass and scythe, yet many years, in which event, he will make much more biography for the second sitting. General Griffith is a gentleman of pleasing address, and his heart is as big as Texas, and as open as his sleeve; of an ardent temperament, he is often impulsive, but never rash nor unjust; his mind is acute, penetrating, and sagacious, and thoroughly analytical in the examination of practical details, while his judgment is clear and perspicuous. In short, General Griffith is a Napoleonic embodiment of restless energy and indomitable will, guided by an equally balanced mind, who would not have occupied a subordinate position in whatever sphere of life his lot had been cast. In the management of his private estate, he has proved himself to be a consummate business manager—commencing with nothing, and having accumulated two fortunes.

In his conduct of the operations of the command at Oakland, Chustenahlah, and Holly Springs, he appeared to the world as a natural-born general, and overlapped West Point in its own peculiar province. As. a legislator, he stood *primus inter pares*, and left the lobby-lined chambers with hands unsmirched and reputation clean. Though unsolicitous for office, and retiring in his disposition, General Griffith would shed honor on the chief magistracy of the State, and his administration of the people's affairs would certainly be in the interest of the people. The following anecdote is illustrative of the General's impetuosity: Upon one occasion he was detailing the exciting scenes attendant upon the Confederate entry into Holly Springs, and especially the earnest welcome extended the rebels by the ladies, when his auditor asked: "And how did you feel, General?" "Feel!" exclaimed the excited veteran; "I felt as if I could have charged hell, and captured the devil, if the Almighty had commanded me to do so!" Of one thing certain, if the General ever does enlist under the banner of the Lord, he will be one of the last to think of giving up the fort, for he goes into every thing with his whole soul—he is never a half-measure man.

As a further testimonial of the regard in which General Griffith was held by his brother-officers, the following letter, from the gallant Jackson, will speak for itself:

"HEAD-QUARTERS FIRST CAVALRY CORPS,
"SPRING HILL, TENN., May 8, 1863.

"LIEUT.-COLONEL J. S. GRIFFITH:

"*Colonel*—Permit me to offer the testimonial of my high appreciation of you as a gallant, competent, and meritorious officer of unexceptional moral character. It affords me great pleasure to refer to the valuable services rendered by your command at Oakland, Mississippi, in repulsing, and routing, a superior force of the enemy, advancing upon Grenada, *and thereby saving our* retreating army; also the gallant and signal service of yourself, while we were together, and commanding separate brigades, on the raid to Holly Springs and West Tennessee. Please accept the assurances of my highest consideration, and with many regrets that your continued ill-health compels you to leave this corps, and a wish that you may soon regain your health sufficiently to enter the service again.

"I remain, very respectfully,
"W. H. JACKSON,
"Brigadier-General Commanding Cavalry Corps."

BIOGRAPHICAL SKETCH

OF

# HON. O. N. HOLLINGSWORTH.

Orlando N. Hollingsworth was born in Calhoun county, Alabama, April 5, 1836, and removed, with his mother, to Rusk county, Texas, in December, 1845, his father having died the earlier part of the last-mentioned year. He laid the foundation of his education in the common schools of the country, and graduated from the University of Virginia, in 1859. He responded, among the earliest, to the call of the South, in 1861, for volunteers, and enlisted as a private soldier in the company of Captain R. H. Cumby, which comprised many of the best young men of Rusk county. His soldierly qualities, and executive capacity, soon secured him promotion to the responsible station of Adjutant of his regiment, the Third Texas Cavalry, in which position he served with credit to himself and profit to the service, until he was seriously wounded in the assault on Corinth, in 1862, and permanently unfitted for service in the field. He returned to Texas, and became interested in the cause of education—a cause in whose behalf he has expended much pecuniary means and the best years of his life. Coronal Institute, located at San Marcos, Texas, was founded by Captain Hollingsworth, in 1864-6, and was long presided over by himself. Subsequently, he was elected Superintendent of Public Instruction, and, on the abolition of that office by constitutional amendment, he was appointed Secretary to the State Board of Education, a position which he now most efficiently fills. In addition to his clerical labors in connection with office, Captain Hollingsworth founded, and conducts, the *Educational Journal*, a timely and invaluable adjunct to the cause that he has espoused. Mr. Hollingsworth is comparatively a young man; has had some experience in practice at the bar, and served one term in the State legislature. Of a benevolent disposition, kind in all his impulses, and highly intellectual, he has always exercised a wholesome, moral influence wherever his services have been required. If merit meets with a just reward, Mr. Hollingsworth may be regarded as a man with a future, and to whatever position he may be called in the service of the State, the people may rest assured of having at least one pure, and honest, and industrious public servant.

BIOGRAPHICAL SKETCH

OF

# COLONEL ELKANAH GREER.

Colonel Greer was born in Marshall county, Mississippi, in the year 1825; received a liberal education, which was just completed at the breaking out of the Mexican war. Though but twenty years of age, he was among the first to volunteer as a private in the First Mississippi Rifles, the colonel of which regiment was Jefferson Davis. Upon the organization of the command, it reported for duty to General Taylor, beyond the Rio Grande. At the battles of Monterey and Buena Vista, in both of which it participated, so signal were its services, that a grateful country expressed admiration for the conduct of both officers and men. Colonel Greer returned home with the regiment on the expiration of their term of service; and, though but twenty-one years of age, was prevailed upon, by his admiring fellow-citizens, to become a candidate for Major-General of militia, defeating General James D. Alcorn, a very popular man, for the position. Under General Greer's control, the militia was organized, drilled, and properly disciplined.

In 1848, he removed to Texas, and soon after, was united in marriage to Miss Anna Holcombe, of Marshall, Texas, eldest daughter of Colonel B. L. and Mrs. Anna Holcombe, a beautiful young lady, possessed of rare charms of both mind and heart. General Greer located at Marshall, and devoted his attention to the civil pursuits of planting and merchandizing. Being an ardent State's rights Democrat, he was deeply interested in the weighty events of 1859 and 1860, which seemed to be culminating into war. General Greer, at this time, probably enjoyed a political influence not surpassed by that of any man in Texas.  He was appointed, in 1859, "Grand Commander" of the secret organization known as the "K. G. C's.," for the State of Texas, and employed himself in the organization of subordinate commanderies throughout the State.  He manfully opposed the conservative policy of Governor Sam Houston, in 1860, and was urgent in his advocacy of a call for a sovereign convention.  Upon the formation of the provisional government, at Montgomery, Alabama, Colonel Greer received the first colonel's commission issued to a Texan, and proceeded immediately to organize the Third Regiment of Texas Cavalry.  Of his services in connection with that regiment, the foregoing narrative speaks.  At the expiration of the first year's service, Colonel Greer declined re-election to the colonelcy of the regiment, though he would have had no opposition (so high was he held in the esteem of the men), and returned to Texas.

Of his services in the Trans-Mississippi Department, the author can not speak.  Colonel Greer was brave, cool in danger, quick to grasp the situation of affairs in the most critical juncture, and as prompt to act.  To these high qualities as an officer, he combined those of the gentleman—kindness and conscientiousness.  Since the conclusion of the war, Colonel Greer has lived quietly, and somewhat retired, upon his estate near Marshall, Texas, respected and loved by his neighbors.

# BIOGRAPHICAL SKETCH

OF

# COLONEL H. P. MABRY.

---

Colonel H. P. Mabry was born in the village of Laurel Hill, Carroll county, Georgia, October 27, 1829. His father, whose Christian name he bears, originally came from North Carolina, settling in Georgia in 1805. He was a soldier in the war of 1812, and in the campaigns against the Creek Indians. The father died while yet the son was but a youth. Young Mabry was deeply impressed with the necessity for an education; and as his patrimony was inconsiderable, he encountered many privations and hardships in the prosecution of his cherished object. After attending this "country-school" for a few months, young Mabry was prepared to enter college—prepared intellectually, but by no means financially. To obviate this difficulty, he entered a store as salesman at a salary of five dollars per month, and in addition to this, he soon found night employment in the post-office. By the most rigid economy, he was enabled, after two years incessant labor, to enter the University of Tennessee, located at Knoxville. Here, by his studious habits and gentlemanly deportment, he won the confidence of the college faculty, and the respect of his fellow-students. But his means were not sufficient to bear him through the entire course, and he was compelled to lay aside his cherished books, and go forth into the world to earn sufficient means to defray his collegiate expenses. Thus did the indomitable boy earn an education by his own industry and perseverance. This indomitable will, and fixedness of purpose, thus early displayed, continued, in after years, to be the most marked characteristics of the man. Not many years after the completion of his education, he removed to Jefferson, Texas, and engaged in mercantile pursuits. In 1854, he was united in marriage to Miss Abbie Haywood—a most estimable lady, worthy to be the wife of a hero—the daughter of W. H. Haywood, Esq., a planter living near Jefferson.

Soon after his marriage, Colonel Mabry commenced the study of law, was admitted to the bar, and at once entered upon a lucrative practice. He was elected to a seat in the Legislature, in 1856, and again in 1859, and was re-elected to the same position, and held a seat in the House of Representatives, in 1861. Upon the secession of Texas, Colonel Mabry returned home, and organized a military company, at the head of which he marched against Fort Wichita. The Federal forces abandoned the fort at his approach, and retired. Captain Mabry occupied the place until May 28, when he was relieved, and, with his company, reported to Colonel Greer for duty, and his company was assigned the position of Company G, in the Third Texas Cavalry, the first regiment that left the State of Texas. As Captain of Company G, and as Colonel of the regiment, the foregoing narrative deals. He was absolutely fearless, and cool to indifference in the midst of danger, and his indomitable will seemed able to grapple with fate itself in the formulation of destiny. He ought to have been a Lieutenant-General, and placed in command of Vicksburg. The "Modern Sphynx" would have found in H. P. Mabry a foeman worthy of his steel. General Robert Toombs, of Georgia, has been credited with the saying, that West Point defeated the Confederacy. Certainly, proven merit did not receive reward by promotion at the hands of Mr. Davis, as justice and the efficiency of the service required. As better illustrating the respect and esteem in which Colonel Mabry was held by those best qualified to judge his merits, the following communications to the Secretary of War are introduced:

"HEAD-QUARTERS, SNYDER'S MILLS,
"YAZOO RIVER, March 30, 1864.
"HON. JAMES A. SEDDON:

"*Sir*—I have the honor to recommend for promotion to the rank of Brigadier-General, P. A. C. S., Colonel H. P. Mabry, Third Regiment, Texas Cavalry; having been near him in the field since July, 1861; having had him under my command, in my brigade, for many months; having seen him tested in camp, on the march, and on various hard-fought fields, I can, unhesitatingly, and do, cheerfully, recommend him for a higher rank, as a meed to merit and distinguished service. He was severely wounded in Missouri, in 1861, and still more severely at the battle of Iuka, on the 19th of September last, when he and his gallant regiment most heroically bore what I considered the brunt of the fight. As a man of correct principles, of soldier-like deportment, of good finished education, of unquestioned coolness, bravery, and sagacity, of systematic and determined character, and as a disciplinarian, I can fully recommend him as highly fitted to take command of a brigade, and I feel sure that his success would be satisfactory to the War Department, the President, and the country.

"I remain, sir, very respectfully your obedient servant,

"LOUIS HEBERT,
Brigadier-General, P. A. C. S."

"HEAD-QUARTERS TEXAS CAVALRY BRIGADE,
"March 27, 1864.

"HON. JAMES A. SEDDON:

"*Sir*—Having learned that the interest of the service demands the appointment of another Brigadier-General in Major-General Lee's Cavalry corps, the undersigned officers of the Texas Brigade cheerfully recommend to your favorable consideration, the peculiar claims of Colonel Mabry, Third Texas Cavalry. He has been faithfully engaged, in the service of his country, since July, 1861; twice severely wounded, and by gallantry and rigid discipline, has won the universal approbation of his superior officers. For force of character, resolution, prudence, indomitable courage, energy, and ability, he has no superior in the cavalry of the Department.

"L. S. ROSS, Brigadier-General.
"E. R. HAWKINS,
"Colonel First Texas Legion.
"D. W. JONES,
"Colonel Ninth Texas Cavalry.
"P. F. ROSS,
"Lieut.-Colonel Sixth Texas Cavalry.
"JILES S. BOGGESS,
"Lieut.-Colonel Third Texas Cavalry."

"HEAD-QUARTERS ARMSTRONG'S DIVISION,
"NEAR CANTON, MISS., March 29, 1864.

"GENERAL S. COOPER,
"Adjutant and Inspector-General, Richmond, Va.:

"*General*—I have the honor to recommend Colonel H. P. Mabry, Third Texas Cavalry, for promotion, to be placed in command of a brigade now in my division. Although Colonel Mabry has never served under my immediate command, I can recommend him, as he commanded a regiment (Third Texas Cavalry, dismounted), in General Hebert's Infantry Brigade, in which I commanded the Third Louisiana Regiment. I consider him an excellent disciplinarian (especially needed in the cavalry), and one of the most competent, in every respect, that can be selected. His regiment, which is the best qualification, is one of the best disciplined, and most efficient, in the service.

"I have the honor to be, with respect, your obedient servant,

"FRANK C. ARMSTRONG,
Brigadier-General."

"HEAD-QUARTERS LEE'S CAVALRY DEPARTMENT,
"CANTON, MISS., March 29, 1864.

"GENERAL S. COOPER,
"Adjutant and Inspector-General, Richmond, Va.:

"*General*—I have the honor to recommend that Colonel H. P. Mabry, Third Texas Cavalry, be appointed Brigadier-General, and assigned to the command of the brigade recently commanded by Brigadier-General Adams. Colonel Mabry entered the service when the war first broke out, and has continued therein ever since, except when temporarily absent on account of two wounds received in battle. I consider him the best disciplinarian in my command. He has distinguished himself in most of the engagements of the West, and has often been complimented for his gallantry and good conduct. I desire Colonel Mabry as a permanent commander of the brigade to which he is now temporarily assigned.

"I am, General, yours respectfully,

"S. D. LEE, Major-General."

"MERIDIAN, MISS., June 23, 1864.

"GENERAL S. COOPER,

"Adjutant and Inspector-General, Richmond, Va.:

"*General*—I have the honor to enclose a return of the brigade commanded by Colonel H. P. Mabry. It is the brigade recently commanded by Brigadier-General Wirt Adams, who now commands a division consisting of the brigades of Generals Gholson and John Scott, in East Louisiana. Mabry's Brigade was in his command, but is now in North Mississippi. General Adams has immediate charge of the country from Grenada to New Orleans. I consider Colonel Mabry one of the best officers I have met in the army, and much desire his promotion. Should it not be deemed proper to appoint him in this Department, and to his present brigade, I trust he may be promoted and assigned elsewhere.

"Yours, respectfully,

"S. D. LEE, Major-General."

# BIOGRAPHICAL SKETCH

OF

# GENERAL J. W. WHITFIELD.

General J. W. Whitfield was born in Williamson county, Tennessee, in the year 1818, and received such limited education as the "log school-houses" of the time afforded. Early in life he pursued the calling of a farmer, but his strong individuality, and marked character, soon called him to public station; and, for eighteen years, with scarce an intermission, he represented his district in both branches of the State Legislature. He served, with marked gallantry, through the Mexican war, and upon its cessation, was appointed Indian Agent to the wild tribes in Kansas. General Whitfield was a resident of Kansas at the inception of the slavery troubles attendant upon the application of that State for admission into the Union, espousing the pro-slavery side of the controversy. Whitfield was the first delegate sent from Kansas to the Federal Congress, defeating the anti-slavery candidate, Reeder, by a handsome majority. In the turbulent era of murder and pillage that ensued, the greater portion of his property was swept away; and when, finally, Kansas was given over to abolitionism, Whitfield, impoverished, removed to Lavaca county, Texas, and resumed the avocation of a farmer. The rude blast of internecine war, however, soon broke upon the quiet scenes of his pastoral life, and the brave old veteran responded by buckling on his sword, and summoning his neighbors to follow him. Starting out as a captain of a company, his command was augmented to a battalion of four companies by the time he reached General McCulloch's quarters. During, and after the campaign that culminated in the battle of Elk Horn, his battalion was increased to a legion of twelve companies, than which, there was not a braver, or more efficient, organization in the Confederate army. General Whitfield relinquished the command of the brigade in 1863, and retired to the Trans-Mississippi Department. In personal appearance, General Whitfield was marked, being over six feet in height, and straight as an arrow—he looked every inch the soldier. Of his services in the Trans-Mississippi Department, the author has no data upon which to predicate a narrative.

After the termination of the war, General Whitfield continued to reside on his farm, near the village of Vienna, in Lavaca county, Texas, engaged in peaceful pursuits through the evening of life, until the autumn of 1879, when he responded to the summons of the specter with the hour-glass and scythe, and took up his solitary march across the river into that undiscovered country in which his departed comrades had pitched their silent camp. There, with Van Dorn, McCulloch, McIntosh, Jones, and others, he awaits the arrival of the rearguard upon the scene to complete the grand re-union of the Texas Brigade, in the shade of the lotus-trees of the Summerland.

BIOGRAPHICAL SKETCH

OF

# COLONEL D. W. JONES.

---

Colonel D. W. Jones was, it is thought, a native Texan, and was born about the year 1842, as he was but eighteen years of age at the commencement of the war.

At the first notes of the approaching storm, he quitted his studies at Maury Institute, Columbia, Tennessee, and proceeded to his home at Mt. Pleasant, Titus county, Texas. He entered the Ninth Texas Cavalry, Colonel W. B. Sims, commanding, it is thought, as a private soldier, and served as such during the first year of the war, through the campaigns in the Indian Territory and in Missouri.

Upon the re-organization of the Ninth Texas regiment, near Corinth, Mississippi, in 1862, though a beardless boy of scarce twenty years of age, D. W. Jones was triumphantly elected Colonel of the regiment; and that he was worthy to be the recipient of this very high honor, the author can bear positive testimony, based upon personal observation.

It was a familiar sight, in the "Army of the West," to see the bronzed and bearded faces of the veterans of the gallant old Ninth following the lead of their handsome and chivalrous boy Colonel. The losses of this regiment were unusually severe, and, at the close of the struggle, nine out of every ten men, who had started, failed to respond at roll-call.

The author again expresses deep regret that he was unable, after the most assiduous efforts, to obtain data upon which to recount the immediate services of the regiment.

Colonel Jones served in the first Constitutional Convention of Texas after the war, and died soon afterward in the city of Houston, where he lies buried in a neglected grave.

Peace to his ashes!

BIOGRAPHICAL SKETCH

OF

# COLONEL JACK WHARTON.

Colonel Jack Wharton was born December 1, 1832, in Washington county, Maryland, and, at an early age, studied law under the celebrated Otho Scott, practicing his profession until 1857, with considerable success in the courts of his native State. At this period, he located in Kansas, where the political feeling was of such a nature, that no Southern man, with any degree of pride for the land of his nativity, could rise in his profession. With all the vim and vitality of a man determined not to be subdued by the passions and prejudices of this eventful period, he started for Salt Lake City, in 1858, with General Harney, who, being ordered back, he left for California under Captain W. S. Hancock—now Major-General—acting as Quartermaster of the Sixth Regiment of Infantry.

After remaining some time in California, he returned to Baltimore, where he remained several months, visiting old friends. It was at this period he established, in Texas, an extensive horse ranche, on the line of Kaufman and Van Zandt counties, about two hundred miles west of Shreveport. Here he remained until the war commenced, when he enlisted, as a private soldier, in a company organized in his neighborhood, and which, subsequently, became attached to the Sixth Texas Cavalry. Upon the definite organization of the company, Wharton was elected Captain. Henceforth, the history of the man, and of the regiment, are indissoluble. He served through all the campaigns, battles, advances, and retreats in which the regiment and brigade were engaged, until the final catastrophe. Upon the appointment of

General L. S. Ross to the rank of Brigadier-General, Wharton, who had been elected Lieutenant-Colonel of the regiment, was promoted to the Colonelcy. After the conclusion of the war, he returned to his stock ranche in Texas, where he remained until 1867, when he was invited by the Southern Pacific Railroad Company, to take charge of their works from Shreveport, Louisiana, to Marshall, Texas, with headquarters at the former place. After the completion of the railroad, he came to New Orleans, where he has resided since 1868.

Colonel Wharton has held many important offices of honor and trust in the State—such as Assessor of Taxes, Secretary of State under Governor Warmouth, Adjutant-General under Governor Kellogg, which place he held until the meeting of the Packard Legislature, when he resigned the office of Adjutant-General, and accepted the position of Clerk of the Superior Civil Court, an office just created, and which was the most lucrative in the gift of the Governor. After the downfall of the Packard Government, he was appointed, by President Hayes, Marshal for the State of Louisiana, from June 15, 1878, which office he holds at the present time, and for four years from the date of commission. Colonel Wharton has an agreeable personal appearance, is a fluent conversationalist, and always a boon companion, and welcomed by *bon vivants*. As an officer in the field, he was surpassed by none in personal courage, sagacity, and devotion. We believe the Colonel never married.

BIOGRAPHICAL SKETCH

OF

# COLONEL JOHN H. BROOCKS.

The subject of this sketch was born in the town of Jackson, county of Madison, State of Tennessee, October 12, A.D., 1829; was the son of the late General Travis G. Broocks—a native of Virginia—and of Mrs. Elizabeth A. Broocks, a native of Alabama. General Broocks removed, with his family, to San Augustine, Texas, in the year 1837. John H. was educated at the Wesleyan College, at San Augustine, and at the San Augustine University. His acquaintance, however, with the practical relations of life, was formed in the counting-room of his father, who did an extensive mercantile business in San Augustine. At the commencement of the Mexican war, young Broocks joined, as a private soldier, the company of Captain O. M. Wheeler, of Colonel Woods' regiment of Texas Cavalry, and rendered efficient services in this new and stirring field of operations until the cessation of hostilities. Returning home, Mr. Broocks entered into the mercantile business at San Augustine, at which place he continued to reside until about the year 1852, when the spirit of adventure and enterprise led him to migrate to California in company of his brother, the late Captain James A. Broocks, and Captain A. D. Edwards, now of Terrell, Texas. In this virgin field, the young Texans first essayed mining, and then worked as hired hands on a hay and small grain farm; and, finally, as merchants, operating under the firm name of J. H. Broocks & Co., at "Shaw's Flat," in Ptoulumne county. While in this business, they did their own freighting with ox-teams, over execrable roads, a distance of sixty-five miles.

Having been quite successful in his business pursuits, Mr. Broocks returned to San Augustine, Texas, in 1854, and was united in marriage to Miss Elizabeth J. Polk. In 1855, he retired from mercantile pursuits to his farm near San Augustine, where he has continued to reside ever since. When Texas called upon her sons to march to battle in defense of constitutional government, in 1861, she found not one more ready to respond to the summons than John H. Broocks. A company was formed in San Augustine, and adjoining counties, of which he was elected Captain. Captain Broocks at once set out at the head of his company to join the army of General Ben McCulloch, in Missouri. Before, or at the time of reaching the army, a battalion was formed of the four detached companies, commanded by Captain J. H. Broocks, Captain J. W. Whitfield, of Lavaca county, Texas, Captain Murphy, of Arkansas, and Captain Brooks, of Arkansas. Captain Whitfield was elected Major of the battalion. Subsequently, Captain Brooks' company was transferred to Colonel McIntosh's Arkansas regiment, and Captain E. R. Hawkins' Texas company joined the battalion. Under this organization, the battalion served in the campaigns against the hostile Indians in the winter of 1861, and at the battle of Elk Horn, in March, 1862. After the campaign in March, an accession of eight more companies was had, and the First Texas Legion was organized with J. W. Whitfield, Colonel; E. R. Hawkins, Lieutenant-Colonel; and ―――― Holman, Major. Major Holman resigned soon after his election, and Captain John H. Broocks was promoted Major. Subsequently, in 1863, Colonel Whitfield was promoted Brigadier-General, Lieutenant-Colonel E. R. Hawkins, Colonel, and Major Broocks, Lieutenant-Colonel. Captain J. T. Whitfield was promoted Major. We reproduce, in this connection, Colonel Broocks' statement in regard to the action at Oakland, Mississippi, as tending to elucidate, in some measure, the account of the same in the body of the narrative.

General Price was retreating from Abbeville, followed by a large supply-train. A considerable force of the enemy was disembarked from transports on the Mississippi river, and by rapid marches, sought to strike the train in flank. Generals Hovey and Washburne, we believe, commanded this expedition, which amounted to about 4,000 infantry, 500 cavalry, and 12 guns. Nothing interposed between the unprotected train and this daring Federal column, but the Texas Brigade of about 1,500 men. Lieutenant-Colonel John S. Griffith, of the Sixth Texas Cavalry, was in temporary command of the brigade.

Colonel Griffith realized the gravity of the situation, and appreciated the value of prompt action. Says Colonel Broocks:

"The Legion, Colonel Hawkins commanding, and three companies as an advance-guard, under my immediate command, fought Washburne's advance fifty-six minutes, near Oakland, Mississippi. We charged, and captured two guns, one of which, only, we brought off the field, as the team attached to the other were killed. Lieutenant-Colonel Griffith, commanding the brigade, was present, and in the charge, bearing himself most gallantly, and but for an accident, we perhaps would have captured Washburne. The Legion was driving the enemy in some confusion. The Sixth Texas had arrived, dismounted, and were ready to join in the fight. The Third Texas, Lieutenant-Colonel J. S. Boggess commanding, had been dispatched to the enemy's rear, and directed to dismount and attack. At this interesting stage, Colonel Griffith received a report (false) that we were being outflanked. Placing credence in the report, he retired his men, and firing ceased. Colonel Boggess, who was just ready to attack in the rear at this time, hearing the firing no more in front, did not attack. Thus an excellently-planned engagement was suffered to pass by default. But the Legions' spirited attack had discomfited the enemy, and, undoubtedly, saved from capture the wagon-train of General Price. Had Colonel Griffith's original plan been carried out, it is probable we would have captured the greater portion of the Federals present. Some idea may be had of the spirited nature of the engagement, from the fact that sixty-four cannon-shots were fired during the fifty-six minutes of action. After we were called off from the charge, the enemy recovered from the confusion caused by our unexpected charge, and their long lines of infantry, 'double-quicking' into position, revealed too much force for Colonel Griffith to again venture an attack."

The enemy accorded the Texans equal respect, and immediately retired from the field, and returned to the protection of their ironclads on the Mississippi river.

Owing to the ill-health of the gallant Hawkins, Colonel Broocks was very often left in command of the Legion, in which responsible station he acquitted himself always with credit, and won the love of his men and the confidence and respect of his superiors in rank. The Confederacy bore upon its rosters the name of no braver, or truer man to its cause, than that of Colonel John H. Broocks. Colonel Broocks has, since the termination of the war, lived a somewhat retired life on his farm, in the midst of his many friends, and surrounded by his interesting family. His name has been repeatedly mentioned in connection with a seat in the State Senate; and, though eminently fitted to grace the councils of State, he has persistently declined the honors which his fellow-citizens would gladly confer, contenting himself with the laborious and unremunerating position of Chairman of the Democratic Congressional District Committee. Colonel Broocks is an educated gentleman—a man of firm will, fixed opinions, and the courage to advocate the same at all proper times. Though it seemed that the moral obliquity of "our army in Flanders" had seized the Confederate army, yet the author can testify to the Roman simplicity and stern exercise of morality by Colonel Broocks, at all times; and never did he hear a profane expression escape his lips. These pages, though in an inadequate manner, testify to the heroism of Colonel Broocks; but of the many high qualities, both of head and heart, of which he is possessed, none may know except those who are drawn into personal contact with him. If heroic services on the battle-field, augmented by capacity, probity, and patriotism, entitle a man to civic preferment, then is Colonel John H. Broocks entitled to the highest office in the gift of the people of Texas. His friend, the author, cheerfully pays this simple tribute to his sterling worth, with the confident hope that he will yet respond to the solicitations of his fellow-citizens, and give to the councils of the State the benefit of his ripe experience, and practical knowledge of men, and political and economical questions.

BIOGRAPHICAL SKETCH

OF

# GENERAL LAURENCE SULLIVAN ROSS.

---

Texas, though her annals be brief, counts upon her "roll of honor" the names of many heros, living and dead. Their splendid services are the inestimable legacies of the past and present, to the future. Of the latter, it is the high prerogative of the State to embalm their names and memories as perpetual examplars to excite the generous emulation of the Texan youth to the latest posterity. Of the former, it is our pleasant province to accord them those honors which their services, in so eminent a degree, entitle them to receive. Few lands, since the days of the "Scottish Chiefs," have furnished material upon which to predicate a Douglas, a Wallace, or a Ravenswood; and the adventure of chivalric enterprise, errant quest of danger, and the personal combat, were relegated, together with the knight's armorial trappings, to the musty archives of "Tower" and "Pantheon," until the Comanche Bedouins of the Texan plains tendered, in bold defiance, the savage gauntlet to the pioneer knights of progress and civilization. And, though her heraldic roll glows with the names of a Houston, a Rusk, Lamar, McCulloch, Hayes, Chevallie, which illumine the pages of her history with an effulgence of glory, Texas never nurtured on her maternal bosom a son of more filial devotion, of more loyal patriotism, or indomitable will to do and dare, than the subject of this brief sketch.

Laurence Sullivan Ross was born in the town of Bentonsport, Iowa, in the year of our Lord, one thousand eight hundred and thirty-eight. His father, Captain S. P. Ross, removed to Texas in 1839, and cast his fortunes with the pioneers who were blazing the pathway of civilization into the wilds of a *terra incognita*, as Texas then was. Captain S. P. Ross was, for many years, pre-eminent as a leader against the implacable savages, who made frequent incursions into the settlements. The duty of repelling these forays usually devolved upon Captain Ross and his neighbors, and, for many years, his company constituted the only bulwark of safety between the feeble colonists and the scalping-knife. The rapacity and treachery of his Comanche and Kiowa foes demanded of Captain Ross sleepless vigilance, acute sagacity, and a will that brooked no obstacle or danger. It was in the performance of this arduous duty that he slew, in single combat, "Big Foot," a Comanche chief of great prowess, and who was for many years the scourge of the early Texas frontier. The services of Captain S. P. Ross are still held in grateful remembrance by the descendants of his compatriots, and his memory will never be suffered to pass away while Texans feel a pride in the sterling worth of the pioneers who laid the foundation of Texas' greatness and glory.

The following incident, as illustrative of the character and spirit of the man and times, is given: "Captain Ross, who had been visiting a neighbor, was returning home, afoot, accompanied by his little son 'Sul,' as the General was familiarly called. When within a half mile of his house, he was surrounded by fifteen or twenty mounted Comanche warriors, who commenced an immediate attack. The Captain, athletic and swift of foot, threw his son on his back, and out-ran their ponies to the house, escaping unhurt amid a perfect shower of arrows."

Such were among the daily experiences of the child, and with such impressions stamped upon the infantile mind, it was but natural that the enthusiastic spirit of the ardent youth should lead him to seek adventures upon the "war-path," similar to those that had signalized his honored father's prowess upon so many occasions. Hence, we find "Sul" Ross, during vacation from his studies at Florence Wesleyan University, Alabama, though scarcely twenty years of age, in command of 135 friendly Indians, co-operating with the United States cavalry against the hostile Comanches. During this campaign the dashing Major Earl Van Dorn led an expedition against the hostiles in the Wichita mountains, which culminated in the hotly-contested battle of the Wichita, in October, 1858. In this engagement, the red warriors of Captain "Sul" Ross, led by their intrepid young white chief, performed prodigies of valor, and to the sagacity, skill, and bravery of Ross was the complete annihilation of the hostiles, in a great measure, attributable. In the moment of victory, Ross was felled to the earth by receiving two dangerous wounds, by a rifle-shot which pierced his arm and side, and was borne from the field on the shields of his faithful and brave Indian retainers. In the heat of the engagement, and before being shot down, Ross discovered a little white girl, a captive, among the Indians. Immediately upon her discovery was her rescue determined upon, and, after a murderous *melee*, was effected. For the particulars of which, as well as of the fortune of "Lizzie Ross," *vide* the concluding pages of this memoir. For conspicuous gallantry on this occasion, Major Van Dorn, upon the field of battle, drew up a recommendation, which was signed by all the officers of the gallant old Second United States Cavalry, addressed to the Secretary of War, asking the promotion of Captain Ross, and his assignment to duty in the regular army. The venerable General Winfield Scott, Commander of the United States Army, wrote an autograph letter to the wounded young leader, complimenting, in the highest terms, the noble qualities displayed on that trying occasion, and tendered him his friendship and assistance. Captain Ross made no attempt to use the recommendation of the United States officers, whatever, but, as soon as his wounds admitted of travel, he returned to college, and graduated in 1859.

Immediately upon his return home, Captain Ross was placed in command of the rangers on the frontier, by appointment of Governor Sam Houston, and repaired forthwith to his post of duty. In December, 1860, at the head of sixty rangers, Captain Ross followed the trail of a large body of Comanches, who had raided through Parker county, to their village on the head-waters of Pease river. Though proverbial for vigilance and cunning, Captain Ross succeeded in effecting a complete surprise, and in the desperate encounter of "war to the knife" that ensued, *nearly all the warriors bit the dust.* So signal a victory had never before been gained over the fierce and warlike Comanches, and ever since that fatal December day, in 1860, the dispirited Comanche "brave" dates the dissipation of that wand of invincibility which it seemed the "Great Spirit" had thrown around them. The blow was as sudden, and as irresistible, as a thunder-bolt from a cloudless sky, and as crushing and remorseless as the hand of fate itself. Ross, sword in hand, led the furious charge of the rangers, and Peta Nocona, chief of the tribe, arose from his last sleep on earth, aroused by the demoniacal saturnalia, in the midst of which his warriors were melting away like snow-flakes on the river's brink, to strike, at least, an avenging blow ere the night of death had drawn its sable curtains around and above his devoted tribe. Singling out Ross, as the most conspicuous of his assailants, with eyes flashing and nerves steeled by the crisis of fate, Peta Nocona rushed on the wings of the wind to this revel of death. The eagle eyes of the young ranger took in the situation at a glance, and he welcomed the redoubtable chief to the contest with a smile. Desperate was this hand-to-hand grapple, for there was no alternative but victory or death. Peta Nocona fell covered with wounds at the feet of his conqueror, and his last sigh was taken up in mournful wailings by the fugitives fleeing from this village of blood and death. Many of these latter perished on the inhospitable plains, in a fruitless endeavor to reach their friends and allies on the head-waters of the Arkansas river. The immediate fruits of this victory were 450 horses and all their accumulated winter supplies. But the subsequent results are not to be computed on the basis of dollars and cents. The spirit of the Comanche was here broken, and to this crushing defeat is to be attributed the pacific conduct of these hitherto implacable foes of the white race during the civil war—a boon to Texas of incalculable value.

It was in this engagement that Captain Ross rescued "Cynthia Ann Parker," after a captivity of twenty-five years, or since the capture of "Parker's Fort," in 1830 (see Thrall's History of Texas, page 455), near the site of the town of Groesbeck, Limestone county. General Ross corrects the statement of Mr. Thrall, to the effect that Cynthia Ann Parker was dressed in male attire, nor was there much doubt as to her identity, as in conversing with her, through the medium of his Mexican servant, who had also been a captive to the Comanches and perfectly conversant with their language, there was but little doubt on the part of Ross as to who his captive really was; and he dispatched a special messenger for her uncle, Colonel Parker. In the meantime, sending Cynthia Ann to Camp Cooper, so that Mrs. Evans, the wife of Captain (afterward Lieutenant-General) N. G. Evans could properly attend to her necessities.

After the carnage had ceased, Captain Ross discovered a little Indian boy lying concealed in the tall grass, expecting, in conformity to the savage customs of his own race, to be killed immediately upon discovery. Ross, with kind words, placed the little fellow upon his horse behind himself, and took him to camp. The little captive was named "Pease," in honor of Governor E. M. Pease. Captain Ross took "Pease" home, and properly cared for him, and he is now with his benefactor, a full-blooded Comanche Indian, though a civilized and educated gentleman.

Captain Ross sent the shield, bow, and lance of Peta Nocona to Governor Houston, who placed them in the archives at Austin, where they now remain, encrusted and stained with his blood. In a letter, recognizing the great service rendered the State by Captain Ross in dealing the Indians this crushing blow, Governor Houston says: "Your success in protecting the frontier gives me great satisfaction. I am satisfied that, with the same opportunities, you would rival, if not excel, the greatest exploits of McCulloch or Jack Hays. Continue to repel, pursue, and punish every body of Indians coming into the State, and the people will not withhold their praise."

But the tempest of sectional hate, that had so long been distracting the country, was now culminating into a seething, whirling cyclone of war, and such a spirit as Ross could not remain confined to the mere border foray, when armed legions were mustering for the titanic strife; he, therefore, tendered his resignation to Governor Houston, who, in recognition of the services rendered by Ross, had appointed him his *aide-de-camp*, with the rank of Colonel. Ross' resignation drew from Governor Houston the following letter, than which a more gratifying testimonial of his worth and services could not be tendered a young man of scarce twenty-three years of age:

"EXECUTIVE DEPARTMENT, AUSTIN, TEXAS,
"February 23, 1861.

"CAPTAIN L. S. ROSS,
"Commanding Texas Rangers:

"*Sir*—Your letter of the 13th, tendering your resignation as Captain in the ranging service of Texas, has been received. The Executive regrets that you should think of resigning your position, as the state of the frontier requires good and efficient officers. He is, therefore, unwilling to accept your resignation. * * * The Executive has always had confidence in your capacity as an officer; and your deportment, as a soldier and gentleman, has met with his entire approval. It is his desire that you at once increase your command to eighty-three, rank and file, and take the field again.

"Very respectfully,

"[Signed] "SAM HOUSTON."

Captain Ross called Governor Clarke's attention to the necessity of entering into treaty stipulations with the Indians on our frontier; and Major Van Dorn also urged the same measure upon the Governor, and suggested Captain Ross as the most proper person to conduct the negotiation on the part of the State, as it was well known he had the full confidence of the "Texas Indians," whom he commanded in the Wichita campaign. In response to these suggestions, Governor Clarke wrote Captain Ross as follows:

"AUSTIN, July 13, 1861.

"CAPTAIN L. S. ROSS:

"*Dear Sir*—When you were here, a few days ago, you spoke to me of the disposition of the Indians to treat with the people of Texas. At the time you did so, I was so crowded with business that I was unable to give to the subject the consideration its importance demanded. I, nevertheless, concluded and determined to adopt and carry out your suggestions. I would be pleased for you to inform me whether it may now be in time to accomplish the objects you spoke of, and, if so, whether you would be willing to undertake its execution. You mentioned, I believe, that a day was fixed by the Indians for the interview, but that you informed them that by that time Texas could not be ready.

"Very respectfully,

"[Signed] "EDWARD CLARKE."

In pursuance of this programme, Captain Ross received his credentials from the Governor, and, taking with him Mr. Downs, of the Waco *Examiner*, and two or three more young friends, set out for the plains. Arriving at Gainsville, Ross met an Indian trader, whom he knew, named Shirley, whose brother was an interpreter, and both of whom lived in the Indian country. He was about to engage the assistance and co-operation of these men, when he learned that General Pike had been commissioned, and was then *en route* to Fort Sill to enter into

LIEUTENANT-COLONEL P. F. ROSS.

treaty stipulations with the Indians, on the part of the Confederate government. Captain Ross, deeming that the interests of Texas could be best subserved by non-action, as certainly all expense and responsibility was obviated, did not attend the interview; nor, indeed, did he allow to transpire the nature of his business in that section, at all, though, through the medium of Shirley, Jones, Bickle, and one or two other white men living with the Indians, all of whom were well known to Ross, the Indians were fully prepared and anxious to enter into friendly relations with the South; so, that when General Pike arrived, the ground lay fair before him, and he found no difficulty in arranging the terms. Captain Ross, who had been in correspondence with the above-named white residents of the Indian section, realized the importance of prompt action on the part of the South, before commissioners of the United States could have opportunities for seducing the Indians from their natural friends. Finding that the Confederacy was moving to the accomplishment of the same object, Ross possessed too much sagacity to invite a conflict of authority between Texas and the Confederacy, as was the case in some other States by a too liberal interpretation of the sovereign prerogative of the States; and, while saving Texas the expense of the negotiation, and all responsibility in the matter, silently contributed to the accomplishment of General Pike's mission. The value of this treaty to the South can not well be overestimated. It not only obviated the necessity for the presence of a considerable force on the frontier which was required elsewhere, but it actually contributed to the augmentation of the Confederate ranks. This great service rendered Texas, and particularly to the immediate frontier, was wholly unselfish and gratuitous, and it is believed the true statement of the case, now, for the first time, finds itself in print. Seeing the consummation of this important affair well under way, Ross returned to Waco and joined, as a private, the company of Captain P. F. Ross, his elder brother. This company was, with others, consolidated into the Sixth Regiment of Texas Cavalry, at the city of Dallas, Texas, and L. S. Ross was elected Major, and commissioned as such September 12th, 1861. In this same regiment, ex-Governor J. W. Throckmorton was Captain of Company "K," and John S. Griffith Lieutenant-Colonel, Colonel B. Warren Stone being the Colonel. The regiment immediately took up the line of march for General Ben McCulloch's army in Missouri. The regiment participated in the battle of Chustenahlah (Creek Nation) with distinguished gallantry, December, 1861, and in the three days' battle at Elk Horn, or Pea Ridge, Arkansas. Just previous to this latter engagement, Major Ross was dispatched upon a raid, at the head of a detachment of about 300 men, composed of companies of the Third and Sixth Texas Cavalry, in the enemy's rear. This delicate expedition, demanding the consummate address of a prompt and decisive commander, was attended with eminent success, General Ross capturing numbers of prisoners and destroying immense quantities of quartermaster and commissary stores.

The "Army of the West," composed of the divisions of the lamented McCulloch and General Price, were transferred to the Cis-Mississippi Department to re-enforce General Beauregard at Corinth, Mississippi, where he was confronted by an overwhelming force of the enemy. The Sixth Texas, as were the other cavalry regiments, was dismounted, and their horses sent to Texas. At Corinth, the command was engaged in a number of outpost affairs until in May, when the first year's service having expired, the regiment was reorganized, and Major L. S. Ross was elected Colonel. Immediately upon his election he was assigned to the command of the brigade in which his regiment was incorporated, in the following order from division head-quarters:

"HEAD-QUARTERS JONES' DIVISION,
May 26, 1862.

"Special Orders No. 11—*Extract.*

"1. Colonel Laurence S. Ross will immediately assume command of Roane's Brigade, Jones' Division, Army of the West.

"By command of

"L. JONES, Major-General,
"CHARLES S. STRINGFELLOW, A. A. G."

Colonel Ross, with his characteristic modesty, declined the honor, and prevailed with General Jones to allow him to remain in command of his own regiment, and General Phifer was subsequently placed in command of the brigade. The summer of 1862 was spent in the camp at Tupelo, Mississippi; the time being principally employed in drilling the regiments, in the case of the dismounted Texans in transforming natural troopers into unwilling infantrymen. The next engagement of importance was the storming of Corinth, and the struggle at Hatchie bridge for the temporary salvation of the "Army of the West." And, as an authorative elucidation of the part borne by Ross and his men, on those two trying occasions, the following letters from General Dabney H. Maury and General Pryor are adduced:

"HEAD-QUARTERS DEPARTMENT OF THE GULF,
"MOBILE, ALABAMA, October 6, 1863.

"MY DEAR COLONEL:

"General Jackson asked me 'to have some colors made for his division. Please send me, at once, the names of the battles in which my old Texas regiments were engaged prior to coming under my command, as I wish to have them placed on their colors. I always think of the behavior of the Texans at Corinth, and at the Hatchie, next day, as entitled to rank with the very "gamest" conduct displayed by any troops in this war. It does not seem to be generally known, but it is a fact, that the fragment of my shattered division withstood the attack of Ord's *corps*, and successfully checked it until the whole train of the army had changed its line of march. For about an hour the remnant of Phifer's Brigade, commanded by Colonel L. S. Ross, held the Hatchie bridge, and with the light batteries, kept the enemy back. Then Cabell's Brigade came up, and the fight was maintained exclusively by my division until we were ordered to retire, which was done in a deliberate and soldierly manner. I often reflect, with satisfaction, on that fight as one of the most creditable to the troops engaged of which I have any knowledge, and I do not believe any thing is known of it outside of the division. No regiment can have a more honorable name upon its flag than "Hatchie," and, to my certain knowledge, no regiment can more justly and proudly bear that name on its colors than the Sixth Texas Cavalry.

"With kind regards, Colonel, I am truly yours,
"[Signed] "DABNEY H. MAURY."

"MEMPHIS, TENNESSEE, June 4, 1867.

"GENERAL L. S. ROSS,
"Waco, Texas:

"*My Dear Sir*—I am requested by General Forrest, who is completely immersed in business connected with a large railroad contract in Arkansas, to acknowledge the receipt of your very esteemed favor of the 21st ult., and to return his, and my own, sincere thanks for your report. You may very well suppose I took great interest in, not only reading your summary of operations while with Forrest, but also in seeing, for the first time, the high testimony General Maury bears to your old regiment at Hatchie bridge. For, you will remember, I was with you, on your staff, on that occasion, and have always taken some little credit to myself for the assistance I was so fortunate as to be able to render to your brigade that day. I was the first to discover that Moore's Brigade, which we had crossed the river to support, as also another command (Whitfield's Legion, I think), had both been scattered, or destroyed as organizations, and that your small brigade, of less than 700 men, was about to be assailed by Hulburt's whole army. I remember that I gained this information from General Moore, whom I accidentally met retiring from the front, all alone on the bank of the river, and immediately communicated to you, with the request of General Moore that you should 'fall back' across the stream, or you would be overwhelmed in ten minutes, or less time, by a force of at least 8,000 men; I remember that you refused, at first, to comply with Moore's request, and sent Captain D. R. Gurley and myself to General Maury for orders, who, upon ascertaining the facts, immediately dispatched you the order to retire. Then, at 'common time,' the brigade was moved by the left flank to the road leading to the bridge (without letting the men know, at first, that they were falling back), when the order to 'file left' was given, and the command brought off in good order, quietly and safely, with the exception of a portion of the extreme right, which, misunderstanding the first order, moved by the 'right flank' instead of the left, and so became separated, and near a hundred of them captured. Withdrawing to the east bank of the Hatchie river, and taking position on a little ridge two or three hundred yards distant, the brigade there made the gallant stand for several hours, to which General Maury so complimentarily alludes. With best regards to my friend Gurley, whom I shall always remember as one of the best and truest, and most efficient of men I ever knew,

"I remain, my dear sir, very truly yours,

"[Signed] "J. A. PRYOR."

But as the foregoing pages of this narrative deals with the services of Ross in the Confederate army, it would be a useless repetition to repeat what has already been said, unless having a direct bearing upon General Ross individually, or tending to illustrate some trait of character.

The defeated Confederate army retreated, via Holly Springs to Grenada, Mississippi, near which place the four Texas regiments were remounted, as already stated. Then came the Holly Springs raid, which forced Grant to retire to Memphis, Tennessee, thus delaying the Vicksburg catastrophe twelve months. Then the march to Tennessee, and the brilliant action at Thompson's Station, in which three thousand of the enemy were captured. Then the long and tedious march to Mississippi for the relief of beleaguered Vicksburg, and the innumerable affairs in the performance of this duty; the fall of Vicksburg and retreat to Jackson, on every foot of which road Ross' Brigade disputed stubbornly the advance of Sherman. The services of Colonel Ross were fully appreciated by his superiors in rank, and he was placed in command of a brigade composed of the First Mississippi Cavalry and the Sixth Texas, and dispatched to the Tennessee valley, conducting a brilliant campaign, against vastly superior forces, by land and river. In testimony of the high appreciation in which they held Colonel Ross, the following testimonial of the officers of the the First Mississippi Cavalry is adduced:

"CAMP FIRST MISSISSIPPI CAVALRY,
"December 21, 1863.

"COLONEL L. S. ROSS:

"The officers of the First Mississippi Cavalry desiring to express their appreciation of you as an officer, have designated the undersigned as a committee to communicate their feelings.

"It is with profound regret that they part with you as their Brigade Commander, and will cherish, with kind remembrance, your generous and courteous conduct toward them, and the gallant bearing you have ever displayed in leading them in battle. The service, with all its hardships and privations, has been rendered pleasant under your direction and leadership. They deplore the circumstances which render it necessary that they should be taken from your command, but feel confident that, in whatever field you may be called upon to serve, the country will know no better or more efficient officer. Our regret is shared by all the men of the regiment, and you carry with you their best wishes for your continued success.

"In conclusion, allow us to say, we are proud to have served under you, and with your gallant Texans, and hope yours, and theirs, and our efforts in behalf of our bleeding country, will at length be crowned with success. Very respectfully,

"W. V. LESTER, Captain Company K.
"J. E. TURNER, Captain Company I.
"J. A. KING, Captain Company G."

Lieutenant-General Stephen D. Lee wrote Mr. Seddon, the Secretary of War, October 2, 1863: "Colonel L. S. Ross is one of the best disciplinarians in the army, and has distinguished himself on many battle-fields, and his promotion and assignment will increase the efficiency of *the most reliable troops under my command.*"

General D. H. Maury wrote from Mobile, Alabama, October 6, 1863: "During the battle of Hatchie, Colonel L. S. Ross commanded his brigade, and evinced such conspicuous gallantry, that, when called upon to report to the War Department the name of the officer who had been especially distinguished there, and at Corinth, I reported the name of Colonel L. S. Ross to General S. Cooper, Adjutant and Inspector-General of the Confederate States Army."

Hon. F. R. Lubbock, while a member of the President's staff at Richmond, Virginia, wrote General Ross: "I have learned, with pride and great satisfaction, of the good behavior, and gallant conduct, and high-bearing of the Texas soldiers, and particularly of Ross' Brigade."

General W. H. Jackson, commanding Cavalry Division, wrote the Secretary of War, October 1, 1863: "I regard Colonel L. S. Ross as one of the best disciplinarians, and one of the most gallant officers, in the 'Army of the West.'"

General Joseph E. Johnston wrote the Secretary of War, October 3, 1863, urging the promotion of Colonel Ross.

All this was done positively without the solicitation of Colonel Ross, and, in point of fact, without his knowledge and consent. The first intimation that Ross had of the honor to be conferred upon him, was the reception of his commission as a Brigadier-General, in the presence of the enemy, before Yazoo City. The appointment sought the man, and there was no one amid all that galaxy of glory, who wore the "wreathed stars" during the stormy period of the war, more deserving the honor than Laurence Sullivan Ross.

We may merely mention the most salient features of the campaigns, henceforth, which, like the rounds of a ladder, bear us, step by step, to the end.

Sherman commenced his memorable march from Vicksburg to Meridian. Ross harrassed his columns in front, rear, and flank incessantly, and retarded the Federal advance until the defeat of Smith's corps, by General Forrest, near West Point, caused Sherman to abandon the idea of marching to Mobile, as he subsequently did to Savannah. Ross was now dispatched, in post-haste, to the Yazoo valley, up which stream a Federal flotilla was ascending, accompanied by a land force of about 3,500 men.

The spirited battles of "Liverpool," "Satartia," and "Yazoo City," were fought, each resulting in a complete victory for Ross, who drove the Federals on board their transports, and, though protected by iron-clad gunboats, drove them down the Yazoo and into Vicksburg. The following testimonial of the citizens of Yazoo City, to the services of Ross and his brigade, is a volume in itself:

"YAZOO CITY, February 6, 1864.

"GENERAL L. S. ROSS:

"We, the undersigned, citizens of Yazoo City, do hereby tender you, and your gallant command, our heartfelt thanks for the noble manner in which you have repelled the enemy, though far superior in numbers, thus saving us from the insults and other indignities which they would have heaped upon us.

"[Signed]: W. H. Mangum, John M. Clark, S. H. Wilson, Alex. Smith, James P. Thomas, Jr., M. P. Dent, R. M. Grail, H. B. Kidd, Mark Berry, S. D. Hightower, F. M. Cassels, John Smith, D. Kearney, R. C. Shepherd, W. L. Stamford, S. C. Goosey, Richard Stephens, S. T. Pierse, F. Barksdale, F. G. Stewart, —— Gibbs, Louis Franklin, J. W. Barnett, C. Hollingsworth, Louis Rosenthral, A. Asher, M. L. Enlich, John Hagman, Jacob Hagman, A. H. Montgomery, Captain O. T. Plummer (Volunteer and Conscript Bureau), Captain W. J. Blackburn (Volunteer and Conscript Bureau), B. J. Harris, James Schmitt, W. Ragster, R. B. Powell, R. R. Callahan, J. O. Dwyer, J. Bradley, C. Swann, Joseph Carr, J. W. Campton, Samuel Goodwin,

J. S. Wallace, Fred. Knabke, John S. Murphy, —— Murphy, J. Mozer, John Reilly, James Carter, James P. O'Reilley, H. C. Tyler, Thomas R. Smith, Hiram Harrison."

The brigade was ordered from the Yazoo section to re-enforce the army of General Johnston, in Georgia. The engagements during this campaign were of almost daily occurrence. Ross' Brigade, at times, constituted a portion of the Confederate line in front of Sherman, and, at other times, was engaged in repelling, fighting, and capturing Federal raiders in the rear of General Johnston's army. In the advance to Nashville, Ross and Armstrong were the eyes of Hood, and, in his defeat and retreat, their two brigades absolutely saved the army from annihilation. But, as has been aptly said, the tide of Confederate success reached its greatest height in Pickett's charge upon Cemetery Heights, and Hood's ephemeral successes were but the spasmodic efforts that precede final dissolution. The end came; and the commencement of the end dates from the day that General Johnston inaugurated his ignoble retreat by retiring from Dalton, Georgia. Had he assumed the offensive there, the Confederacy would have been spared the sad catastrophe that befell it.

It is not pleasant to contemplate these heroic men struggling against an iliad of woes. They had borne their banners on the highest waves of victory, and stood as conquerors on the Ohio itself. Now, foot-sore and weary, ragged, famished, after nine-tenths of their numbers had been offered as sacrifices upon the altar of duty, they stood contemplating the inevitable. The rest is known of all.

General Ross returned to his home, near Waco, and, with his interesting family, lived the quiet and honorable life of a farmer. Since his twentieth year, he had shared all the vicissitudes of a soldier's life. The golden morning of life had been spent, without the hope of fee or reward, in the arduous duties and dangers of the battle-field. He now sought repose, content to remain on

> "The Sabine farm, amid contiguous hills,
> Remote from honors and their kindred ills."

But, in 1873, his friends called him from retirement by electing him Sheriff of McLennan county. In this position he remained several years, and so efficient were his services, that he was styled, by those who had opportunities for judging, "The model Sheriff of Texas!" Voluntarily retiring from office, he again sought the privacy of his country home. In 1875, he was elected a member of the Constitutional Convention that framed the present organic law of Texas. As tending to illustrate, in some degree, the part borne by General Ross, and the policies advocated by him in the prosecution of this grave duty, a few extracts are reproduced from the leading journals of the time. The Waco *Daily Telephone*, of November 8, 1877, in a rather hostile review of the Constitution, and especially of Article V. (the Judiciary), says:

"Judge Ballinger and General Ross protested against their action (the "Rutabagas"), but were overslaughed. * * * * Our readers will remember the unanswerable argument of General Ross against the reduction of the judges, salaries, and judicial districts, against which the "Rutabagas" opposed—not their arguments, but their votes."

The *State Gazette*, Colonel John D. Elliott, editor, said:

"We can never refer to the name of General Ross without feeling an inspiration of admiration scarcely ever equaled in our experience of life. He is one of nature's noblemen—as artless and unostentatious as a child, as courageous and heroic as ever bore the image of man, and as able as the ablest of the land. His record in the Constitutional Convention showed him as exalted a patriot and statesman as the man of letters and thorough representative of the people. He is eminently fitted for the highest trust of the Commonwealth. We know of no citizen of the State who would add greater luster in her chief magistracy than General Sul Ross."

The following letter is from the pen of Colonel John Henry Brown, and appeared in the columns of the Dallas *Morning Call*:

"*Another Richmond!—A Good Man for Governor—Enthusiastic Suggestion of General Sul Ross, of Waco.*—A soldier-boy on the frontier—a leader of Indian scouts under Van Dorn while yet a youth—the gallant boy Captain who rescued Cynthia Ann Parker after twenty-five years captivity—a private soldier winning his way up to a Brigadier-Generalship—the hero of more than a hundred battles and fights—the modest and educated gentleman—for five years the model Sheriff of the State, and in the Constitutional Convention displaying the highest qualities of eloquence and enlightened statesmanship—why may not his thousands of friends present his name for the position of Chief Magistrate of the State he has so nobly, and ably, and disinterestedly served since he was thirteen years old? Why not? He has never intimated such a wish; but his friends claim the right to mention his name. Ask the people of the whole frontier—ask the people of his large district—ask his neighbors—ask the thirty thousand ex-soldiers who know his deeds, and see what they all say. They will send up one grand shout for Sul Ross."

All of which the *Telephone* endorsed in the following language:

"General Ross' sound, practical abilities, are unquestioned, and few men are more justly esteemed. We believe he would fill any position which he consents to accept, with ability, faithfulness, and dignity. We do not know, however, that he would consent to become an aspirant, at this time, for the gubernatorial office. We do know, however, that he will never intrigue or scheme for the position; and, if tendered the nomination, it will be a voluntary offering by the State at large, without reference to local or personal predilections and efforts. Under those circumstances, General Ross would make a Governor equal to any Texas ever had."

Such, in brief, is a hasty synopsis of the life of General L. S. Ross. The foregoing pages of this narrative attempt to elaborate some of the incidents in his career that won for himself the confidence of his superiors in rank, and for his brigade the encomium of all. Nothing like a complete history of Ross, or his brigade, is claimed here. At this late day, in the absence of all documentary material to use in the construction, that desideratum is impossible of attainment; and, with the conclusion drawing nigh, the author feels like exclaiming: The half has not been told; and the fragment here preserved falls far short of doing the subject justice! Probably, no general officer who commanded troops in the late war, drew them in closer sympathy to himself than General Ross. Each man of his brigade regarded his dashing young chieftain as a personal friend. As Junot was prompt to resent a fancied insult to Napoleon, so would the troopers of Ross have drawn their sabers at any allusion disparaging to their idolized leader. Brave unto rashness himself—*he had seven horses shot under him in the course of the war*—yet he was solicitous of the welfare of his men, and all his plans of attack or defense contained, in an eminent degree, the element of prudence. Often, with his skeleton brigade, he seemed tempting the wrath of the Fates, and as risking all upon a single cast of the die; but no mission of danger ever appalled his men, for, following his dashing and seemingly reckless lead, they again and again plucked "the flower safety from the nettle danger."

In the disastrous retreat of Hood from Nashville, the brigades of Ross and Armstrong were the palladiums of hope to the discomfited army; and had it not been for their interposing shields, Hood's army, as an organization, would have ceased to exist ere a passage of the Tennessee river could have been attained.

A characteristic letter from the General's pen will conclude this sketch of his life—a letter written in the expectation that no eye save the author's would ever scan its pages—as tending to illustrate somewhat those noble qualities of heart that so endeared him to his men. The noble sentiments expressed are characteristic of the man.

General Ross was recently elected to a seat in the State Senate, distancing his competitor by an unparalleled majority, and running two thousand votes ahead of his own party ticket. Apropos to General Ross' opposition to the "Judicial Article" of the State Constitution, it is gratifying to his friends to know that five years of experience has demonstrated his wisdom in pronouncing the article, on the floor of the Convention, "wholly inadequate to meet the wants of the great State of Texas, and that, as a system, it must prove in the end more expensive than the one sought to be displaced." As the Democratic party in convention at Dallas demands, through the "platform," an amendment to the Constitution to meet this particular want, a more emphatic and unqualified vindication of General Ross' course in the Constitutional Convention could not be framed.

"WACO, TEXAS.

"VICTOR M. ROSE,
  "Victoria, Texas:

"*My Dear Friend*—Your kind letter did not reach me promptly, but I hasten to assure you of my approval of the commendable work you design. You will probably remember that, during the war, Captain Dunn, whose health had failed, detailed to write a full and accurate history of the operations of the brigade, and I furnished him with all necessary data—orders, papers, etc.—so as to render his duty of easy compliance; but, unfortunately, he died in Alabama, and this information was received, together with that, that my trunk and papers entrusted to his care had fallen into the hands of the enemy. In my trunk was found twenty stands of colors, and other trophies which we had captured from the Federals. My memory is too defective to be relied upon at this late day for much valuable information, but such as I can trust, I will gladly give you; and I feel warranted in saying, that Captain Gurley, and others of our comrades, will aid you in your noble work, which, I trust, you will not delay for the endorsement of any one.

"I was glad to hear from you. Indeed, every few days, by letters or calls from my noble, brave boys, am I assured that they remember me kindly. No churchman ever loved to tell his beads as I love to recount their valor and their loyalty in the discharge of a solemnly-conceived duty. Long after I was thoroughly satisfied they knew they were being called upon to follow a "will o' the wisp" to their utter discomfiture—naked, footsore, and famished as they were, yet, with heroic devotion, they met every peril unflinchingly, and encountered every hardship unmurmuringly. I hope steps will be taken soon to bring about a happy reunion of all those who are still living, and then we can take steps to honor and embalm the memory of the dead.

"I would be pleased to have suggestions from any, or all, of our comrades everywhere, as to the practicability of getting up some kind of an organization, and I am ready to concur in any plan devised. My health is not very good. I contracted a cold from exposure in the Mississippi swamp when we were crossing over those arms, and it eventually settled on my lungs, and from that time I have suffered much from bronchitis, and have often thought consumption would ensue. I am farming, and making enough to provide for the wants of myself and wife, and six children. Happily, my early training upon the frontier, among the early pioneers of Texas, inculcated no very extravagant desires. Please remember me to all my "boys," and tell them that if we are never permitted to meet *en masse* on this earth, when we "cross over the river" we shall enjoy a grand and glorious reunion, and have a long, long time to talk it all over.

"Very truly your friend,

"[Signed]           "L. S. ROSS."

# BATTLE OF THE WICHITA.

### THE RESCUE OF LIZZIE ROSS FROM CAPTIVITY.

Ross' faithful Indian scouts reported the discovery of a Comanche village near the Wichita mountains, and, immediately, Major Van Dorn set the column in motion (including Ross' command), and, by a fatiguing forced march all night, came in the immediate vicinity of the village just at break of day. A reconnoisance showed that the wily Comanches were not apprehensive of an attack, and were sleeping in fancied security. The horses of the tribe were grazing near the outskirts of the village, and consisted of a *caballado* of about five hundred head. Major Van Dorn directed Captain Ross, at the head of his Indians, to "cut off" the horses, and drive them from the camp, which was effected speedily, and thus the Comanches were forced to fight on foot—a proceeding extremely harrowing to the proud warriors' feelings.

Just as the sun was peeping above the eastern horizon, Van Dorn charged the upper end of the village, while Ross' command, in conjunction with a detachment of United States Cavalry, charged the lower. The village was strung out along the banks of a branch for several hundred yards. The morning was very foggy, and, after a few moments of firing, the smoke and fog became so dense that objects at but a short distance could be distinguished only with great difficulty. The Comanches fought with absolute desperation, and contended for every advantage, as their women and children, and all their possessions, were in peril.

A few moments after the engagement became general, Ross discovered a number of Comanches running down to the branch, about one hundred and fifty yards from the village, and concluded that they were beating a retreat. Immediately, Ross, Lieutenant Van Camp, of the United States Army, Alexander, a "regular" soldier, and one Caddo Indian, of Ross' command, ran to the point with the intention of intercepting them. Arriving, it was discovered that the fugitives were the women and children. In a moment, another posse of women and children came running immediately past the squad of Ross, who, discovering a little white girl among the number, made his Caddo Indian grab her as she was passing. The little pale-face—apparently about twelve years of age—was badly frightened at finding herself a captive to a strange Indian and stranger white men, and was hard to manage at first.

Ross now discovered, through the fog and smoke of battle, that a band of some twenty-five Comanche warriors had cut his small party off from communication with Van Dorn, and were bearing immediately down upon them. They shot Lieutenant Van Camp through the heart, killing him ere he could fire his double-barreled shot-gun. Alexander, the United States cavalryman, was likewise shot down before he could fire his gun (a rifle). Ross was armed with a Sharpe's rifle, and attempted to fire upon the exultant red devils, but the cap snapped. "Mohee," a Comanche warrior, seized Alexander's rifle, and shot Ross down. The indomitable young ranger fell upon the side on which his pistol was borne, and, though partially paralyzed by the shot, he turned himself, and was getting his pistol out, when "Mohee" drew his butcher-knife, and started toward his prostrate foe—some fifteen feet away—with the evident design of stabbing and scalping him. He made but a few steps, however, when one of his companions cried out something in the Comanche tongue, which was a signal to the band, and they broke away in confusion. "Mohee" ran about twenty steps, when a wire-cartridge, containing nine buckshot, fired from a gun in the hands of Lieutenant James Majors (afterward a Confederate General), struck him between the shoulders, and he fell forward on his face, dead. "Mohee" was an old acquaintance of Ross, as the latter had seen him frequently at his father's post on the frontier, and recognized him as soon as their eyes met. The faithful Caddo held on to the little girl throughout this desperate *melee*, and, strange to relate, neither were harmed. The Caddo, doubtless, owed his escape to the fact that the Comanches were fearful of wounding or killing the little girl. This whole scene transpired in a few moments, and Captain N. G. Evans' company of the Second United States Cavalry, had taken possession of the lower end of the Comanche village, and Major Van Dorn held the upper, and the Comanches were running into the hills and brush; not, however, before an infuriated

Comanche shot the gallant Van Dorn with an arrow. Van Dorn fell, and it was supposed that he was mortally wounded. In consequence of their wounds, the two chieftains were compelled to remain on the battle-ground five or six days. After the expiration of this time, Ross' Indians made a "litter," after their fashion, borne between two gentle mules, and in it placed their heroic and beloved "boy Captain," and set out for the settlements at Fort Belknap. When this mode of conveyance would become too painful by reason of the rough, broken nature of the country, these brave Caddos—whose race and history are but synonyms of courage and fidelity—would vie with each other in bearing the burden upon their own shoulders. At Camp Radziminski, occupied by United States forces, an ambulance was obtained, and the remainder of the journey made with comparative comfort. Major Van Dorn was also conveyed to Radziminski. He speedily recovered of his wounds, and soon made another brilliant campaign against the Comanches. Ross recovered sufficiently in a few weeks so as to be able to return to college at Florence, Alabama, where he completed his studies, and graduated in 1859.

The little girl captive—of whose parentage or history nothing could be ascertained, though strenuous efforts were made—was named by her benefactor, "*Lizzie* Ross," in honor of Miss *Lizzie* Tinsley, daughter of Dr. D. R. Tinsley, of Waco. The sentiments that prompted the chivalric ranger in this selection of a name, will soon be discovered to the reader.

The soldier, Alexander, recovered of his wound in the course of several months, but of the brave fellow's subsequent career, the author knows nothing.

General Ross, after the expiration of twenty-two years since the battle of the Wichita, said to the author; "I shall never forget the feelings of horror that took possession of me when I saw the arrow sent clear up to the *feather* into the body and heart of the gallant young Van Camp, who, I think, belonged to the Engineers, and only accompanied Major Van Dorn in the capacity of a volunteer *aid*. I then thought but little of my own danger, but expected, of course, that my time had come to balance accounts."

Of Lizzie Ross (we will anticipate the thread of the narrative), it can be said that, in her career, is afforded a thorough verification of Lord Byron's saying: "Truth is stranger than fiction!" She was adopted by her brave and generous captor, properly reared and educated, and became a beautiful and accomplished woman. Here were sufficient romance and vicissitude, in the brief career of a little maiden, to have tuned the "roundelay's" of "troubadour and mennesanger." A solitary lily, blooming amidst the wildest grasses of the desert plains. A little Indian girl in all save the Caucasian's conscious stamp of superiority. Torn from home, perhaps, amid the heart-rending scenes of rapine, torture, and death. A stranger to race and lineage—stranger even to the tongue in which a mother's lullaby was breathed. Affiliating with these wild Ishmaelites of the prairie—a Comanche in all things save the intuitive premonition *that she was not of them!* Finally, redeemed from a captivity worse than death by a knight entitled to rank, for all time in the history of Texas, *primus inter pares.*

Lizzie Ross accompanied General Ross' mother on a visit to the State of California, a few years since, and while there, became the wife of a wealthy merchant near Los Angeles, where she now resides, the queen of a happy household, surrounded by all things that render life attractive or desirable.

Such is the romantic story of Lizzie Ross—a story that derives additional interest because of the fact of its absolute truth in all respects.

General Ross was united in marriage to Miss Lizzie Tinsley, of Waco. Mrs. Ross is a lady of sterling qualities of mind and heart, and, in all respects, a congenial companion of her heroic husband. The union has been blessed by six children; and now, in the midst of the peaceful quiet that surrounds his happy home, the General, doubtless, beguiles the tedium of *ennui* by recounting to his "young brigade" the exploits of his old. The latter are descending the hill of life toward the setting sun, in obedience to the distant sound of the final tattoo that comes from beyond the western hills; the former, lit by the aureole of his rising glories, are responding to the morning reveille with youth, and health, and hope. May their paths be the paths of peace; and if the trade of war *must* be pursued, may it never be the tocsin of internecine strife that shall summon them to the field of carnage and death. No bloody chasm now divides the Gray and Blue! A reunited people commands the peace of sections! These are the tidings of great joy to the people of the American Union—one indissoluble whole of indestructible States! And so may it ever be, "For we be brethren!"

# REMINISCENCES OF CAMP CHASE.

Kilpatrick succeeded in getting away from Lovejoy Station with about thirty or forty of the Texas Brigade, among whom are now remembered: Captain Noble; Lieutenants Teague, Moon and West; Privates Crabtree, Pirtle, Nidever, Mapes, "Major" White, Reuben White, Fluellen, and Ware. The march of the prisoners to the lines of General Sherman was fatiguing in the extreme. The Confederates had been in the saddle for three consecutive days, during which time they had partaken of not one regular meal; and the Union troopers were almost as destitute of rations, though what little they had was generously divided with their famished prisoners. The prisoners were well treated by their captors. It was only the "home guard" who delighted in misusing these unfortunates of war, just as the professional politician on either side refuses even now to be placated. The men who confronted each other in battle were too brave to feel pleasure in inflicting pain on a prisoner. The braves of Hancock, Custer, McClellan, and Rosecranz are not the men who have kept the "bloody shirt" waving; nor are the men of Joe Johnston, Beauregard, Maxy, and Ross, found among the impracticables, who, like his excellency, the late President Jeff. Davis, imagine the Confederacy still exists. General Sherman's convention with General Johnston expressed the sentiments of the soldiers on either side. Arriving at Sherman's quarters the prisoners were placed in the "bull-pen," and given a "square" meal of "hard-tack" and "sow-belly," as crackers and bacon were called by the Federals. In the "bull-pen" were a number of whining, canting, oath-seeking hypocrites and sycophants, who, with the characteristic zeal of new converts, employed their time in maligning every thing connected with their suffering section, and in extolling the superior civilization of the North. The fiery and impetuous Crabtree could not brook this despicable servility, and he undertook to do battle, singly and alone, in vindication of the South. A lively "scrimmage" was on the tapis, Crabtree knocking his opponents right and left, when the guard interposed on behalf of the new converts, whom every brave Unionist secretly despised. After a day or two spent here, the prisoners were placed on the cars and conveyed to Nashville. Here the forlorn fellows were placed in the yard of the penitentiary, and kept for several days, as General Wheeler was in the vicinity with a large force of cavalry, and a rescue was feared. Finally, by rail again, the prisoners were taken to Louisville, Kentucky. Upon entering the guard-house, each prisoner was required to deposit, in a large tub near the door, his pocket-knife, money, and whatever else of value he possessed. No account whatever was taken of the articles so confiscated, nor did the prisoners ever hear of their property again, or compensation for the same. The journey from Kentucky's metropolis, through Cincinnati and Columbus, to Camp Chase, distant four miles from the capital of Ohio, was without incident, save the escape of Lieutenant A. J. West, of the Sixth Texas. Some time before reaching Louisville, and while the cars were flying at the rate of forty miles an hour, the night being intensely dark, this daring young officer jumped from the train, and, strange to say, suffered no accident or injury from the rash leap. He made his way through the enemy's lines in safety to his own command.

Camp Chase was situated near the Sciota river, so said, for, during the author's sojourn of near nine months in those delectable quarters, he had no opportunity for observation beyond the prison walls. The "Camp" consisted of three "prisons," designated respectively, "No. 1," "No. 2," and "No. 3." In "No. 1" officers exclusively were confined, "No's 2 and 3" accommodated the twenty or thirty thousand privates on hand—a number sufficient to have averted the catastrophe at Petersburg. The "prisons" were enclosed by a plank-wall upwards of fifteen feet high. On the top of this wall a guard, consisting of about twenty "posts," was stationed, with doubtless another line on the outside below, as certainly a heavy "relief" was always immediately on hand. A slight ditch, or furrow, on the inside of the wall, and parallel with it, was the "dead-line," over which no "Reb" might venture, unless desirous of making himself the target of the vigilant guard. The quarters of the prisoners consisted of comfortable frame buildings in two rows, and fronting upon a common street. The houses were capable of containing near two hundred prisoners. Bunks in tiers of three formed the sleeping accommodations. Colonel W. P. Richardson commanded the post, and Lieutenant Sankey was Provost Marshal. The rations consisted of three crackers and about four ounces of white fish per day. Sometimes the bill of fare was varied by the issuance of beef and flour, but not in quantities exceeding the above estimate. In consequence of such short rations, the prisoners were constantly experiencing the pangs of hunger, and that some died absolutely of sheer starvation, the writer is indubitably certain. Three men occupied a bunk, and sometimes during the night one would die, when not unfrequently the remaining two would actually contend over the corpse for his rations and blankets. Men here—many—lost all self-respect, and the worst passions of our nature predominated over the good. Though the prisoners were not allowed money, yet they were given "sutler's checks" in lieu, ranging in denominations from five to fifty cents. The sutler's shop abutted against the wall, and through a crevice, about three inches wide and six in length, a prisoner, blessed with the possession of these coveted checks, could purchase stationery, needles and thread, gutta-percha buttons, tobacco, and a few other immaterial articles. Anything, however, in the nature of provisions or clothing was under the severest ban. Nothing eatable entered the prison walls save the meager rations doled out to the half-famished men. Many of the prisoners, addicted to the use of tobacco, would occasionally sell one meal per day for five cents, with which to purchase a half-dozen chews of the weed. In this way a considerable trade sprang up, and several prisoners conducted quite a grocery business. One, a Georgian, Waddell of name, earned quite a considerable little sum of money. The old skin-flint converted his bunk into a store, and here higgled with the starving wretches who brought their rations to exchange with him for a small piece of tobacco, or extolled the flavor of the same rations to some would-be purchaser who had the "sutler's checks" to pay for the luxury.

Robberies were not unfrequent, and an incorrigible Englishman—who was the subject of quite a voluminous correspondence between Lord Lyons and Mr. Seward—was frequently punished. This wretch was sometimes fastened to a cross, and his face laid directly under the spout of the pump, though the weather was bitter cold, and the water pumped into his face until respiration would be suspended. At other times, he was placed in a barrel having holes through which the arms protruded, and in this novel jacket he would be compelled to "mark time" in the snow for hours.

The author remembers meeting in prison No. 2, a young Illinoisan, who represented himself as the county judge at Paris, Illinois, imprisoned simply because he was accused of being a "copperhead."

To add to the calamities of the wretched men, the small-pox broke out among them, and from twenty to thirty of the poor fellows were carried out in rude coffins each morning to the "silent camping-ground." Of the small company of Texans, Reuben White and Al. Nidever died.

An old Frenchman is remembered—they called him "Old Bragg," who had been blown up at Vicksburg with the gallant Third Louisiana Regiment, and captured. "Old Bragg" had one leg missing, one arm and one eye gone, and the poor old fellow's mind was sadly impaired. His whole thought was bent upon an exchange of prisoners, and each morning he would arise at daylight from his hard bunk and announce: "Boys, ze exchange he come to-day; zay tell me so last night!" and forthwith he he would begin to pack up his scanty effects and hobble to the prison gate, where he would remain the greater portion of the day in expectation of being called to commence the glad journey to his sun-kissed Louisiana. This was his programme, without material variation, for several months. The poor old fellow finally died before the "exchange came," and sleeps in that silent camp, with thousands of his comrades, in the midst of a people who have no flowers to strew upon the rebel's grave.

It may be noted that quite an industry sprung up in the manufacture of gutta-percha rings and other trinkets, which went to swell the traffic of old Waddell.

About the only diversion afforded within the walls was in walking around the camp, and, thus engaged, could be seen thousands of aimless men, unless the desire to "kill time" be an aim, walking around and around the camp like tigers, bears, and lions in their cages.

The author can not refrain from acknowledging the kindness of a fellow-prisoner, Mr. John D. Miller, of Victoria, Texas, who, though in a separate prison, managed to convey some of the desired checks to him. And, though lucre is not unwelcomed at any time, this certainly was the most heartily welcomed and thoroughly appreciated of any ever received, before or since.

Thus the winter passed. The spring came. Lincoln's brutal assassination startled the prisoners, and the surrender of Lee destroyed the last vestige of lingering hope. Applicants for the oath now became so numerous, and, as they were treated with such contempt by the "reb to the last," that it was deemed best to separate them, giving the rebs prison No. 3, and the "razor-backs," as the applicants for the oath were called, prison No. 2. About this time Colonel Hawkins, of Tennessee, gained access to prison No. 3, and made the boys a brief, but eloquent, "talk," concluding: "Remain true to the cause of Dixie; and, if our worst fears are realized, we can be able to say with King Francis at Pavia, 'All is lost but honor.'" This manly utterance was applauded by the ragged, half-starved patriots to the echo.

Finally the "exchange came," though poor "Old Bragg" slept too soundly to hear the summons, and the prisoners were conveyed south in batches of 500. The squad in which the author left proceeded by rail to Cairo, and thence down the Mississippi river to New Orleans. At Cairo, the kind-hearted citizens vied with each other in their contributions to the necessities of the miserable Southerners.

Without disembarking at New Orleans at all, the prisoners were steamed back to Vicksburg, and here disembarked under the auspices of a negro guard. This was the most humiliating experience of the whole period of captivity. The noble ladies of Vicksburg interested themselves in ministering to the necessities of the Confederates. The Texans were especially indebted to Miss Nora Roach—whom to call an angel, is but to compliment the saintly host that ministers around the "great white throne." At Vicksburg, Ross' *miserables* were paroled, and soon *en route* for their Texan homes.

The Unionists, while heaping merited censure on the Confederate authorities for the mal-treatment of Federal prisoners at Andersonville, and other Southern prisons, deny the charge of mistreatment of Confederate prisoners themselves. In support of what is here stated as being the rule at Camp Chase, from September, 1864, until May, 1865, the author refers to any truthful Confederate there confined within the period specified. They could not have been treated worse and live, for many absolutely died of starvation. An exchange of prisoners was demanded in the interest of humanity. The Washington administration refused to sign a cartel, because it would give the South what she most needed—men. The Confederacy was unable to properly feed her own soldiers in the field. The Washington administration were well advised of this fact, yet it allowed Union prisoners to die of ill-treatment, when one word pronounced by Lincoln and his advisers, would have freed them. Posterity will judge correctly who is responsible for the graves at Camp Chase, Camp Douglas, Rock Island, Andersonville, Richmond, and other pens North and South.

---

NOTE.—During the trying days in Camp Chase, there were some who never relaxed in their fealty to the South, and who never forgot that they were gentlemen. Among these it is a pleasure to name James Arnold, Sixth Texas Cavalry, now of Wartrace, Tennessee; James Crabtree, J. D. White, Perry Pirtle, William Fluellen, of the Third Texas Cavalry, and John D. Miller, of Victoria, Texas.

## THE SOUTH.

#### VICTOR M. ROSE.

### I.

She hath doff'd the weeds of her widowhood,
  To resume the trappings of pride;
In the midst of the festive and gay she stood,
  With the mien of a willing bride.

### II.

She hath smiled on the suit of a stranger knight
  Whose progress admits of no pause;
But e'er in her heart a memorial light,
  Burns on for the dear Lost Cause.

### III.

O, loyal and true in her heart of hearts,
  As the fealty demanded above;
But the Union restored of segregate parts,
  Must divide with the dead her love.

www.ingramcontent.com/pod-product-compliance
Lightning Source LLC
Chambersburg PA
CBHW032133160426
43197CB00008B/627